RAISING

CONFIDENT

CHILDREN

A Guide for Parents and Teachers

By

Pat Guy

ISBN-13: 978-1-8382927-0-6
BOBBY PUBLISHING

For Holly, Amy, Toby, Ruby, Jamie, Theo, and Reuben.

CONTENTS

CHAPTER 1

THE EARLY YEARS

INTRODUCTION

'Give me a child until he is seven and I will show you the man.'

This quote from Aristotle (often attributed to Francis Xavier, one of the founders of the Jesuit Order), makes reference to the influence of early experience in the development of a child's character. The human baby learns to stand, to talk, and to think in a period of three or four years. The baby does this without formal instruction through instinct and imitation. The young child will mimic the behaviour of those around them: the attitudes and values of their family and carers will be absorbed and used as a blueprint for the adult that the child becomes.

1. FAMILIES AND CONFIDENT CHILDREN

a. 'In his master's steps he trod.' (Good King Wenceslas.)

John Bowlby proposed his 'Attachment Theory' in 1958. Bowlby's theory describes young children's innate drive to establish a strong attachment with their main carer(s). This need to attach to particular adults can be explained in evolutionary terms as any young animal that enjoyed close ties with an adult animal would be protected and more likely to survive to maturity.

Provision of care outside the family for pre-school children has expanded rapidly over the last generation. In 1981, 24% of women returned to work within a year of giving birth. In 2010, 76% of mothers returned to work within 12 months of having a child. Currently in the UK, there are approximately 23,500 day-nurseries and 9,600 pre-schools. 277,000 children under three are enrolled in day-nurseries, and nearly a quarter of all babies and toddlers under two years of age spend some time in nursery care.

In their election manifesto of November 2019, the Liberal Democrat Party offered working families 35 hours per week of free childcare for children from nine months to two years, over 48 weeks of the year.

I wonder if these babies and toddlers will go on holiday during their four weeks annual leave. My daughter once worked on cruise ships in the Caribbean. She was astonished to discover that the 'Kiddies' Care Club' ran throughout all ten days of every cruise, from 7.00 a.m. to 7.00 p.m., and was always fully booked. Kiddies' Care Club on Christmas Day being booked up months in advance.

Charles Dickens wrote 'A Christmas Carol' in 1843. The main character, a miserly businessman called Ebenezer Scrooge, has no empathy for anyone, no matter how desperate their situation. In the story, Scrooge is visited by three ghosts. The first ghost takes Scrooge back to his childhood at boarding school, reminding him of how he was left at the school by his father during the Christmas holidays. Did this lack of affection from his own family, so early in his life, contribute in some way to Scrooge's lack of compassion for others?

Some parents have to return to work after the birth of their baby for financial reasons, other parents for reasons relating to career progression. Some couples want to have a family, but to continue to pursue their own interests.

My friend's daughter recently described a local children's park to me: the extensive green spaces, the different climbing frames, and brand-new swings, slides, and sandpits in the playground areas. I asked if her toddler enjoyed going there. She replied that she hadn't taken her daughter there, because the child was now in nursery full-time. She had seen the park through the window while using the rowing machine at the gym. I couldn't help but wonder if her daughter might be saying something similar in the future: 'I saw Mum today. I drove past the care home, looked out of the car window and there she was, sitting in the porch, almost as if she was waiting for someone to take her out. I'm sure the matron said they entertain them in-house.'

b. Raising confident children

'Whether you think you can, or you think you can't – you're right.'
(Henry Ford. Ford Motor Company.)

There are strong links between confidence and well-being. Confident children are less concerned about the opinions of others, and less likely to react to peer or media pressure. Confident children tend to be social magnets because they're fun to be around. For these children situations are never hopeless, just problems to be solved: they will look for answers, rather than be frozen by anxiety.

When confidence is so desirable, how can parents help their children to develop self-belief? Key strategies would include:

<u>To remember that children need adults' time and attention</u>. Sir Anthony Seldon, former Head of Wellington College, and one of the first Headteachers to introduce well-being lessons into the classroom, emphasises the vital role that families play in children's healthy development. 'Families are the best schools for the development of character. When children are nurtured in loving, caring homes, they have the best possible start in life.'

<u>To remember that children are individuals, with different interests and rates of development.</u> Comparisons to siblings or peers are unpleasant. Just because an older brother walked, talked and took his GCSEs at 8 months/14 months/nine years of age, does not mean that his siblings will. Life is not a race. No one in their right mind would want to be first over that particular finishing line.

<u>To remember that children copy our actions and not our words</u>. Adults should set an example. There is no point in chilling on the sofa watching a box set, quaffing a few cans of lager, and then ridiculing your son for not getting into the school football team. Children copy their parents' behaviour.

I have the ability to speak in voices, and most of them are my mother's.

c. Self-efficacy

When a child feels that they have little control over their lives, they are said to experience <u>learned helplessness</u>. The child will not act to help themselves in challenging circumstances, because they feel there is no point; they 'know' they will be unable to improve the situation. Everyone will feel like this sometimes, but when a child always feels helpless, they are likely to develop a pessimistic outlook on life.

Self-efficacy refers to the individual's confidence in their ability to deal with challenges. Children with high levels of self-efficacy will see problems as linked to external factors, specific to particular situations, and only temporary. If these children fail a test, they will assume that the test must have been particularly difficult, but their failure doesn't mean they will do badly next time, or if tested in a different subject. They will assume that if they work harder or more effectively, they will be able to improve their performance.

To encourage children to develop self-efficacy:

- Let the children decide which activities they would like to be involved in, rather than imposing activities on them.

  'My Dad is Chair of the local rugby club and he wants me to play rugby for the club's junior squad. I don't want to because they have to train so hard. I want to spend my weekends hanging out with my friends.'

  'My Mum wants me to go to after-school netball, but I don't like netball. I want to come home after school, and not have to wait for the late bus.'

  'My PE teacher says I will need to go to training twice a week if I want to be in the school swimming squad. I like swimming, but not that much.'

- Help them to move on from disappointment or frustration. Not to waste time ruminating over what went wrong, but to use their time to plan what to do next.

- Encourage the child to think in shades of grey, rather than black and white.

- If the child feels upset and irritated, help them to use those emotions to galvanise themselves into action.

- Avoid the use of words such as 'never' and 'always', when

describing their performance.

- Suggest the child views failure in terms of a lack of effort, rather than a lack of ability. If they spend more time revising or revise more effectively, they will do better next time. This sort of approach to disappointment has been shown to reduce children's feelings of helplessness.

d. How to develop a child's self-confidence

Children with high levels of self-confidence will have better mental health. Self-confident individuals will be less concerned about the opinions of others, while children who need approval from their peers will be more susceptible to self-doubt and anxiety.

Ways to help children develop their confidence:

- Help the child to work out how to do a task. How to mend a bike, revise for a test, or to learn this week's spellings. How to organise themselves, clean their shoes, and manage their time. If a child feels they have the skills necessary to tackle tasks, their self-confidence will improve.

- Encourage the children to do more of what they enjoy, as well as anything they're good at. Practice will improve their performance in these areas and have a positive effect on their self-esteem.

- Praise effort and bravery as well as talent. Children who lack confidence may be too frightened to try anything different or new, because they are afraid of failing. This will have a cumulative effect, as they will be unable to build on previous successes. If the child has overcome apprehension before, they will have that experience to refer back to: 'I didn't think I'd be able to give the talk to the new Year 7s, but then I remembered feeling like that before I did the reading at the Carol Concert, and that turned out OK.'

- Be open when you struggle with something to show that difficulties and problem-solving are a part of everyday life. Use such phrases as: 'Oh well, I'll just have to have another go.' 'Nothing ventured, nothing gained.' 'Maybe next time.' 'Nothing is ever perfect the first time you do it.' 'I'll try again later.'

- Demonstrate confidence in the children and make it clear that you believe they are capable of completing a task. Build up their confidence through a small-step approach to tasks in order to minimise the effect of any setbacks. Then, even if something does go wrong, you can point out all the things that went right.

- Helping others will help the child to feel better about themselves: perhaps by being more considerate towards neighbours, walking the dog, helping older family members, and being loyal to their friends. Any positive feedback the child receives from others will boost their confidence.

- Encourage the children to participate within the school community: volunteering to play with younger children at break, running extra-curricular clubs, joining the School Council, helping to coach sports teams, or working with the Librarian at lunchtime. When a child is respected and valued by others, they will be able to respect and value themselves.

- Encourage the children to join social groups and clubs within the wider community: local choirs, sports clubs, amateur dramatics, and church groups, or babysitting circles. A range of talents and competences will be a confidence-booster for any child.

e. Confident body language

Once, while attending a job interview at a prestigious girls' independent school, I was shown round the school by two sixth-formers, who then fed back to the interview panel. I wasn't short-listed for the position because (or so the Headteacher would have had me believe), the sixth-formers found me rather scary. Any child who knows me would laugh out loud at the idea of anyone finding me 'rather scary'. However, this goes to show how important body language is as a method of communication. Communication is 7% of what is said, 38% tone of voice and 55% body language.

I am not alone in appearing to be something I am not. Many children have problems with their body language, in addition to reading the body language of others. The child may come across as shy, aggressive, arrogant or unfriendly, when they are none of these things.

It is worth pointing out the basics of body language to increase children's understanding of how they might appear to others.

To appear confident. To appear confident, act as if you are. Stand up straight with your head up and feet planted firmly on the ground, relax your shoulders, lower the pitch of your voice, and speak steadily.

To appear friendly and approachable. Keep still and relaxed. Look others in the eye when starting a conversation, just for long enough to identify their eye colour. Always leave space between you and the other person (about a metre), or they may feel uncomfortable. Avoid fidgeting when listening to others, as this will give them the impression that you are bored or nervous. Smile at them and they will automatically smile back … or run. Decide on the brilliance of your smile by how much you like the person. You do not have to like everyone.

Meanwhile, I plan to continue to appear scary. It has always bought me a couple of lesson's peace before I am rumbled.

2. CHILD DEVELOPMENT

a. Piaget's stages of child development

Jean Piaget (1896-1980) was a Swiss psychologist who carried out extensive research into child development. Piaget devised a staged model to demonstrate how children's knowledge and understanding of the world develops. The stages of development are the same for every child.

1.   The sensori-motor stage (Birth to 2 years)

From birth to 2 years of age a baby is always on the go, constantly moving and exploring the world through their senses by, for example, putting everything into their mouths.

2.   The pre-operational stage (2 years to 7 years)

In the pre-operational stage, the child develops more abstract ways of thinking through imitation, play, and language. Although their use of language will be improving, they will still think in concrete terms. During this stage, the child only understands the world through their own eyes and will find it hard to understand how others feel.

3.   The concrete-operational stage (7 years to 11 years)

During this stage, the child acquires the ability to apply rules to objects, such as height and weight. Their thinking becomes more logical, rational, and organised, although their understanding is still based in the real, rather than the theoretical, world.

4.   The formal operational stage (11 years to adult).

During the formal operational stage, children begin to use logic to understand abstract ideas and solve problems.

b.   Understanding child development

It is vital that schools and educational policy-makers do not inadvertently create problems for children. The stage of a child's neurological and emotional development will be more relevant to their behaviour and performance than their chronological age. There will be significant differences in levels of development between children of the same age, and all young children's needs should be considered on a child-by-child basis.

Most children will take their first steps between the ages of 9 and 14 months. The average child will start to walk between the ages of 10 and 20 months. Most children will be potty trained between 18 months and 3.5 years of age. The average child will be dry at night between 3.5 and 6 years of age.

The compulsory school starting age in England and Cyprus is five years, six in Italy and the Netherlands, and seven in Sweden, Poland, and Finland.

Most English children will start their Reception Year in the September preceding their 5th birthday. Early years experts advocate play-based provision in the first years of school, with formal schooling delayed until the age of 7.

Ofsted's report, 'Bold Beginnings', of November 2017, highlighted the need for increased collaboration between Reception and Year 1 classes, in order to prepare the children for 'proper' school. This was seen as an opportunity to introduce formal teaching methods at an earlier stage, rather than an opportunity to extend play-based learning into later school years. However, teaching children skills before they are physically and intellectually ready simply does not work, and the children are likely to become disheartened and demoralised.

Fun pre-reading and pre-number activities can be enjoyed by children in the early years, ensuring that they are ready to develop literacy and numeracy skills in due course, rather than trying to leapfrog the development of underlying competences in order to accelerate the children's progress. There is no hurry: any advantage gained from an early start in reading and writing will soon disappear, and the children who start to learn to read and write later will quickly catch up.

Research has linked negative early school experience with mental health problems and concluded that the reduction in opportunities for free play, and an increased focus on academic achievement in recent years, have had a significant impact on children's well-being.

Children do not need challenging and over-stimulating environments: they need generous amounts of interaction with their family, to be properly fed, cared for emotionally, and allowed to play.

c. Maslow's Hierarchy of Needs

American psychologist, Abraham Maslow, produced his 'Hierarchy of Human Needs' in 1943. The Hierarchy describes five stages of sequential need that must be met before an individual is able to reach their full potential.

Stage 1. Physiological Needs. Food, water, warmth, sleep, and shelter. Once the child's needs at stage one are met, the child can progress to stage two, and so on.

Stage 2. The need for safety and security. The security and protection of a family and a home.

Stage 3. The need for love and a sense of belonging. Nurturing caregivers, positive emotional relationships, and secure friendship groups.

Stage 4. Self-Acceptance. Feelings of self-worth and accomplishment.

Stage 5. Self-Actualisation. Reaching one's potential.

Maslow's Hierarchy was instrumental in focusing attention on the importance of meeting children's basic need for love and security.

d. Summer birthdays

Children are legally required to start school at the beginning of the term following their fifth birthday. Parents of children with birthdays that fall in the summer term between April and August can request a delayed start to the Reception Year for their child. They can choose to start the child in a Reception class a year later, in the September following their fifth, rather than fourth birthday.

The chronological age of the child and the long-term implications of relative immaturity need to be considered on a child-by-child basis.

In 2017, data showed that 45% of young footballers in Premier League academies were born at the beginning of the school year in September, October, and November, and 10% were born at the end of the school year in June, July, and August. Boys born at the beginning of the school year will be physically more mature than those born at the end of the school year. They will be taller, stronger, and faster, and so more likely to be chosen to play for class and school teams; they will go to more team practices and be involved in more matches against other schools. This additional practice will lead to a virtuous circle in terms of improved performance. The advantages of physical maturity in children's sport are easy to understand, so it would seem sensible to also consider the effects of the month of a child's birth on their academic performance.

Children born in the summer months have always been at a disadvantage at school, with some of their classmates being nearly a year older, but changes to the age at which children start school, and the pressure on schools to introduce formal learning to ever younger year groups, have aggravated this situation. It has always been the case that some children will have an extra year in primary school, but in the past, the leapfrogging of the year would happen in Year 3 or Year 4, after the children had established basic literacy and numeracy skills.

Many four year olds, particularly those with a summer birthday, in Reception classes will be incapable of sitting still for long enough to follow instructions, or paying attention and listening quietly without fidgeting and involving themselves in other activities. This is not through a deficiency on the child's part, but a question of physical and mental maturity over which the child has no control.

f. Early language development

Language acquisition starts early in life and babies tune into the rhythm and sounds of language from birth. It is important to talk with babies, even when they appear to be too young to respond.

To help young children with the development of language:

- ✓ Maintain eye contact while you speak, so the child realises that the sounds you are making are directed towards them.

- ✓ Reduce unnecessary noise. If you have the TV or radio on, the child may be unable to distinguish your speech from this background noise. Adults can automatically block out one sound to concentrate on another. The fact that the radio is on will not affect their focus when talking on the phone. Young children find this selective attention much more difficult.

✓ Point out interesting things when out for a walk. When the child speaks, perhaps pointing out a dog in the street, respond and add a few extra words.

'Dog. Dog.'

'Yes, what a tiny dog. Ahh, look at him wagging his tail.'

✓ Talk to the child in different situations: as you cook breakfast, hang out washing, go shopping, or pick up older children from school.

'Oh look, there's Jamie. He's playing football with his friends. I wonder if he's seen us?'

✓ Nursery rhymes provide the perfect input of rhythmic language, with short simple phrases and lots of repetition. Clapping along to the rhymes reinforces the pattern of the sounds. 'Baa, baa, black sheep.' 'Sing a song of sixpence.' 'Hickory dickory dock.' 'Pat-a-cake, pat-a-cake.'

✓ Read books with the child. Stories that have repeated phrases are particularly appropriate. 'Trip, trap, trip, trap over the...' 'I'll huff and I'll puff...' 'Run, run, as fast as you can...'

✓ Rather than correct a child's speech, repeat what they have said in the correct way.

Child: 'He helloed me.'

Adult: 'Yes. He said hello to you. What a kind dog.'

✓ Use music to help the child to pick up the rhythms and tones of sound. Lots of singing and music activity sessions are held at local libraries, toddler groups, and play centres.

✓ Attend all appointments for hearing checks. Temporary or permanent hearing loss will affect the development of language.

g. Children are only children

Let's hit the ground running, give 110%, and take it to the next level. Many parents work in high-pressure environments where they are judged by their productivity. Every waking and working moment must be maximised.

'Professional' parents will approach child rearing in the same way. If they become aware of any shortcomings in their child's skillset, they will put compensatory strategies into place immediately, in the same way that they would support an under-performing work colleague. Time is tight, and the desired outcome must be achieved as quickly as possible therefore, for example, the children will have one-to-one swimming instruction before school, rather than going to the swimming pool at the weekend with their family to play and have fun.

Parental insecurity is easily turned into hard cash. Parents will pay for their children to get an edge over others, taking additional music, ballet, drama, and language lessons from an early age.

(These before- and after-school classes also provide a guilt-free child-minding service, enabling parents to cram a few more hours in at the office or the gym.)

Children will be expected to build their CVs through academic achievement and participation in a range of extra-curricular activities.

Unfortunately, encouraging children to view all hobbies and interests in terms of, 'Would this look good on my UCAS personal statement?', will reduce the likelihood of the child pursuing anything purely for pleasure.

When children's after-school hours are filled with additional tutoring, ukulele lessons and obscure language courses, the time available for relaxation and the type of imaginative and physical play essential for the development of their creativity, social skills, and secure mental health will be reduced. Children do not develop into well-rounded individuals through gruelling hot housing.

e. Why play is important for children

Why is play so important for children? Play is the way in which all young animals are programmed to learn, and children are no different. Depriving children of time for free play will disrupt their social, emotional, physical, and intellectual development.

Play assists social development

When children play together, they learn how to work as a group, how to share, compromise, negotiate with others, and solve disagreements. Children do not learn in a second-hand way. They will not learn social rules from an adult telling them how to behave, but from interacting with their friends, and working out what is acceptable behaviour and what is not.

Play develops children's physical ability

Play develops children's gross motor skills because of the opportunities it gives for physical movement: running, climbing, skipping, swinging, jumping, and throwing. Young children will play ball with their friends in the park for hours just because it is fun. As they play, they will hone their throwing, catching, kicking, and batting skills far more than would be possible at an organised sports class.

A child's fine motor skills and hand-eye co-ordination will be developed though play activities that involve painting, modelling, building, cutting, sewing, pasting, threading, and colouring.

Play allows children to burn off energy

Young children can only sit still and pay attention for short periods of time before they need to move. Physical play provides an outlet for children's natural energy and exuberance.

Play allows children to explore the lives of others

Pretend play gives children the opportunity to explore the lives of others, and to develop empathy. When children are involved in make-believe play, they will have the chance to understand how it feels to be a parent, bus driver, family pet, baby, teacher or superhero.

Free play develops children's language

Children will need to explain themselves clearly during imaginative play. They will have to communicate with their peers about people and objects that are not physically present. 'Which rocket are you going to fly? The red one or the blue one? My rocket can swim. What can your rocket do?'

Pretend play can be therapeutic

Imaginative play can help children deal with difficult situations. The children can act out situations that are troubling them, or events that they have enjoyed and would like to re-live. Having a birthday party, getting their hair cut, a new baby in the family, Christmas celebrations, or starting school. As the child is in control of the play, they can stop the action if they become frightened or apprehensive and change the end result in their favour.

Play lays the foundations for abstract and theoretical learning

Play is not the opposite of work; play complements work. It is essential that all early learning is practical and based in the child's own experience. Young children do not acquire knowledge and understanding in a second-hand way.

When children play on their bikes, they will learn the fundamentals of force and motion. Playing with sand and water will help them to understand the principles of mass and volume. Playing outside will develop the children's appreciation of the natural world.

Play allows children to think creatively

Children can work together to devise their own games and think creatively to adapt the rules or context of a game to fit their purpose.

Free play allows children to be absorbed in their own interests for long periods of time

When children play and become engrossed in their own world, they are refining their skills and increasing their knowledge base, as well as having fun. They may roller skate in every spare moment, draw picture after picture of cartoon characters, or play make-believe games with soft toys. Any activity that gives the child pleasure will ensure they understands how it feels to feel happy and engaged.

Play gives children time to relax

All young children need down time to relax, day-dream, mess about, and even, God forbid, to be bored. All children like to play alone sometimes; they do not need constant amusement or adult engagement.

3. WELL-BEING

a. What is well-being?

The level of an individual's well-being is a measure of how they feel about their life. Are they generally happy and healthy, with a positive outlook? Children with high levels of well-being are more likely to enjoy life, have a wide circle of friends, and not let stress or difficulties overwhelm them.

Having a good sense of wellbeing does not mean that the child is continually happy, but that they are able to cope successfully with different emotions: sadness, happiness, frustration, loneliness, and anxiety, whilst continuing to maintain a balanced outlook on life.

b. Stress in childhood, and how to cause it

YoungMinds, the children's mental health charity, reports that nearly one million children between the ages of five and fifteen years experience mental health problems. This anxiety does not relate to real-world issues – war, poverty, global warming, conservation, or national security – but derives from sources closer to home.

Factors that cause children anxiety include

Pressure at school. The NSPCC found academic worries to be a cause of stress for 50% of children. School work can drain away free time; and homework commitments leave children with little time to play or relax. When children have less free time and expectations of them are high, even mundane problems will be magnified and harder to manage.

Changes to traditional family support networks

Changes within society have led to the development of a variety of different family types. Many families are now 'blended'. A blended family is formed when parents end one relationship and then re-partner to form a new family unit. These new family groups will include the children from previous relationships. The breakdown of the original family group will be difficult for the children to accept, and linking with another family may reduce the opportunities for support from child's biological relatives: grandparents, aunts, uncles, cousins, and siblings.

Over-use of social media

On social media sites everyone appears to be happy and enjoying themselves with friends and family, the equivalent of a 1980s Round Robin Christmas card constantly dropping through your letter box. (Dictionary definition of a Round Robin = a generic letter sent to relatives and friends, usually at Christmas, telling the recipients what you had done that year.) Round Robins used to be a source of amusement, as the recipient would know the sender and understand the letter to be more exaggerated highlights than an accurate reflection of the sender's daily life. By contrast, the individuals on social media sites will not be known to the child, and the child will have no way of knowing if their posts are true, exaggerated, or works of pure fiction.

Early exposure to adult issues

My seven-year-old granddaughter came home from school recently and announced that she was bi-sexual. Her mother assumed that some form of gender diversity lesson must have taken place and asked the child why she thought she might be that way inclined. My granddaughter replied that it was because she thought Fleur, her best friend, was pretty.

It is easy to see how my granddaughter's conclusion would have been reached. The children are told that some girls find other girls attractive, and that these girls are called bi-sexual. Therefore, if you're a seven-year-old and you think your best friend is pretty, you must be bi-sexual. Nuances of adult sexuality are too confusing to discuss before a child is old enough to have a grasp of the basics, with all of the hazy euphemisms used by adults open to childish interpretation.

Standards of physical beauty

Not only are children under pressure to perform well in school, and to be popular with their peers; they must also be physically attractive. Being judged on your physical appearance used to be a female-only problem, but now is an issue for all.

The current definition of attractiveness is very narrow and, as a result, many young people will feel insecure about their appearance.

Two children per week were referred to the NHS for possible gender reassignment in 2009. By 2019 this number had risen to fifty per week.

The percentage of girls within this group increased by 4,400% in the ten years between 2008 and 2018. (Penny Mordaunt. Minister for Women and Equalities. 2019)

Female body types, personalities, interests, and behaviours exist across a broad spectrum, and the representation of females in the media does not reflect this diversity. Girls can be six foot four with a 32A cup; use minimal makeup; enjoy playing darts, Minecraft, cricket or bass guitar; wear size 10 shoes; choose Physics, Computer Studies, Statistics, and Chemistry for their 'A' levels; want to be in the armed forces, a car mechanic or work on an oil rig, without the need for them, (or anyone else), to question their gender or sexuality.

When girls are counselled over body image anxiety, I do hope they are supported by real women; women without fake tans, botoxed brows, plumped and pouting lips, eyelash extensions, breast and buttock implants, false nails, or veneered teeth. Girls are a diverse group, and much more than Lara Croft clones.

c. Sensitive children

Some children are naturally more sensitive than their peers. They are hyper-responsive to their environment and become upset and worried by situations that other children are able to manage without thought. Their responses to life events can be extreme and emotional.

Sensitive children will need much 'more of the same' by way of good parenting and empathetic support in school:

1. Routine and predictability. All children will thrive on stability and predictability, but for these children routine is essential.

2. Consistently high levels of affection from family and carers.

3. Regular and generous opportunities for imaginative play.

4. Supported challenge to extend their comfort zones in a sympathetic way.

5. An acceptance of the child for what they are and a recognition of their personality, quirks and all.

d. Positive thinking. How to help children to deal with stress

Positive psychology focuses on the positive emotions of everyday life: happiness, love, gratitude, resilience, and compassion. While psychologists would typically analyse what is going wrong for an individual, positive psychology is the study of what is going right.

Helping children to deal with stress: -

- Teach children to count their blessings, to be grateful for what they have and compare themselves to those who have less, rather than yearn for more, and compare themselves to those who do. My friend volunteers for the Age Concern charity and recently visited Kathleen, an eighty-five-year-old widow. Kathleen has diabetes and a heart condition that restricts the distance she is able to walk. She was hoping to find a residential placement in local sheltered accommodation, so that she could socialise more, but, as she told my friend, she was one of the lucky ones, because she didn't have that dementia like some poor souls.

- Make enough time for children to do things they enjoy: playing in the garden; going to the park, swimming pool or cinema; being with their family or out with their friends. When they are feeling happy and positive, they will see problems as challenges, rather than threats.

- Creative activities (painting, drawing, sewing, creative writing, crafts) have been shown to help children distract themselves from stressful situations.

- Show the child how to focus in the present and consider the reality of a situation, rather than what they think might be happening. Not to brood over negative events, but shift their attention to alternative, more pleasant thoughts.

- Demonstrate positivity as an adult. Things go wrong for everyone sometimes, but the situation will never be hopeless. Children need parents and carers who are calm, unflappable problem solvers.

- Explain that nobody really knows exactly what to do or how to behave. Everyone feels insecure and worried sometimes, even if they appear self-assured. No matter how confident and outgoing, or how marvellous someone's life appears to be, they are certain to experience upset and disappointment.

- Keep the children fit and healthy. Stress can be relieved in the short term through exercise. Go for walks, runs, bike rides, or play in the garden. Getting out into the natural world, parks, and green spaces is known to promote mental health and feelings of well-being.

- Explain to the child that things can go wrong for anyone. Watch the news or look at newspapers, particularly the sports pages, for everyday embarrassing clangers in international sporting events: dropping an easy catch, missing an open goal, or a player tripping over their own feet. These sportsmen and women have to acknowledge their mistakes, 'suck it up', and move on.

- Teach the child to see setbacks as minor, temporary hiccups and something they can deal with. Even when some aspects of a situation are beyond their influence, there will be small steps they can take to increase their level of control.

- Yoga, meditation, and mindfulness will provide the child with opportunities for quiet reflection. Mindfulness can be described as on-going meditation, in which the child pays close attention to everything they are doing, and everything that is happening in that particular moment. Mindfulness is acknowledged as a useful way to detach from negative or stressful thoughts.

- Encourage the child to be kind to others and considerate towards to their peers. Kind behaviour attracts kind behaviour.

- Help the child to develop and maintain different social circles: friends from school, church groups, sports clubs, voluntary associations, or their local neighbourhood. This will give the child access to different support networks.

- Encourage the child to develop positive friendships. Friendships that are two-way, constructive, and encouraging, rather than ones that drain the child's energy and enthusiasm.

- Teach the children to view social media with a degree of scepticism.

- Help children to talk about their feelings. Everyone experiences similar challenges in life and will be able to give advice or have alternative ideas of how problems could be tackled. Close relationships with others will provide the child with emotional support and reduce any feelings of isolation.

- Demonstrate how to devise a plan of action, rather than sit and worry. Worrying will make problems circulate in the child's mind, whereas planning possible solutions will re-focus their attention. Help the child to take control of a situation, rather than allow the situation to take control of them. They should accept what has happened, identify the problem, think of a few possible solutions, choose one solution, and work out how to follow it through.

The Australian Psychological Society carried out a well-being survey in 2015 to discover how successful different ways of dealing with stress were felt to be by the interviewees. They identified six most frequently recommended approaches:

1. Spending time with family and friends.

2. Doing something physically active.

3. Getting involved in a hobby or interest.

4. Listening to music.

5. Focusing on the positive.

6. Getting out into the natural world.

e. Well-being and sport

Sport offers children choice from a huge diversity of activities. Every child will be able to find at least one sport they enjoy and can use for relaxation, socialising, and to develop their self-esteem.

Sport will support children's well-being in numerous ways:

✓ Sport relieves stress

The hormones released when a child feels anxious will be burned off during exercise rather than staying in the body and causing headaches, stomach aches, and other physical symptoms.

✓ Sport protects self-esteem

Spending their free time playing sport has been shown to reduce the amount of time children spend on-line. Young people whose social lives revolve around social media sites are more likely to worry about the opinions of others than children who have real-life contacts and interests.

✓ <u>Playing sport develops self-regulation</u>

Sport will help a child to develop self-control. A member of the opposition may fool the umpire into awarding their team an advantage, but the child will know that they cannot let one injustice deter them, or have a negative impact on their overall performance.

✓ <u>Sport encourages children to be courageous and try new things</u>

The fear of looking silly can stop children from doing anything new, but trying different approaches and learning from errors will teach athletes valuable lessons. Dick Fosbury, an American high jumper, start to experiment with new and unusual high jump techniques while he was still at school. The 'Fosbury Flop' is now the jumping technique used by all serious high jumpers.

✓ <u>Sport gives children experience of dealing with failure</u>

Life is competitive. Sport gives children an experience of failure, but in manageable doses: losing a running race in the garden with siblings, losing a school hockey match, or an inter-class tennis match. The ability to bounce back from disappointment is essential at all levels of sport.

✓ <u>Sport helps children to develop delayed gratification</u>

Sport places an emphasis on training the mind as well as the body. The child will have to exert self-discipline in order to achieve long-term goals.

✓ <u>Sport gives children opportunities to extend friendship groups</u>

Sports clubs offer the perfect environment for establishing friendships with others who have similar interests. Children involved in sport outside school will have different sets of like-minded friends.

✓ <u>Participation in sport promotes a healthy lifestyle</u>

When children are interested in sport, they will be aware of issues relating to health and fitness, knowledgeable about what constitutes a good diet, and the dangers of smoking, drug use, excessive drinking, and a sedentary lifestyle. When children are members of sports clubs, they will be surrounded by positive role models who take their physical health and fitness seriously.

✓ <u>Sport can provide different levels of challenge</u>

The child can choose their level of challenge: some children will enjoy extreme sports, physical challenge and overcoming fear. Participating in such activities will increase their confidence in other situations. Other individuals will gain a sense of satisfaction from perfecting the skill of diving from the side of a swimming pool for fifty years.

A sport can become a lifetime hobby, benefitting the child socially, emotionally, and physically, so it is vital that participation and fun is not hijacked by adult ambition. Many children are 'talent spotted' at an early age. Their parents send them to junior squad training camps and extra coaching sessions, without realising the broad trawl for talent that such identification involves. Let the child participate in sport for fun, rather than risk their enthusiasm for football, cricket, tennis, gymnastics, or athletics fading in a blur of intensive professional training, competitive selection procedures, high-stake matches, and unnecessary injuries.

<u>f. 'Sleep is the best meditation.' (The Dalai Lama)</u>

When children do not get enough sleep, they will be irritable and find it hard to concentrate and focus. School-aged children need between eight and eleven hours sleep each night. Older children will need slightly less than younger ones.

The deepest periods of sleep occur during the first few hours. It is at this time that children's brains produce growth hormone. During later periods of sleep, memory and learning are consolidated.

To help children with sleep:

❖ Try to increase the amount of exercise the children do during the day so that they feel physically tired. Walking or cycling to and from school and being out in the fresh air will help. If the child is mentally tired from working all day in a stuffy classroom, but still has physical energy to burn, they will find it harder to settle at night.

❖ One of the benefits of outdoor exercise is exposure to natural light. Natural light is the most powerful and ingrained regulator of human sleep patterns. Our ancient ancestors would sleep when it was dark and wake when it was light.

❖ Make sure the children's bedrooms are cool and well ventilated. Close the curtains and keep the room as quiet and dark as possible.

❖ Do not give the children a large meal immediately before sleeping. Bananas are believed to promote and sustain sleep and would provide a suitable healthy snack.

❖ Stick to a pre-bedtime routine. Try to make the routine as unhurried as possible to give the child enough time to wind down gradually: bath, a milky drink or snack, bedtime story, lights out.

❖ Avoid fizzy drinks and junk food before bedtime. Additives and caffeine will reduce the likelihood of falling asleep easily.

❖ Do not let the children watch frightening or exciting DVDs immediately before going to bed, or to use social media in their bedrooms. The artificial light from screens and phones will confuse their brains into thinking it is day. Gossiping on social media with friends will give the child things to think about and mull over before they can relax.

4. FAMILY LIFE

a. Children want to conform. Choose your child's name with care.

One of the most exciting things about becoming a parent is choosing your child's name. Traditional or modern? Family name or quirky? What may seem a cute name for a baby may not suit the adult the baby grows into. I know a Grace, Hercules, Angel, and Temperance who are anything but.

Many parents' choice will be based on their feelings about their own names. My husband's preference was for mainstream-conventional, while I opted for short and sweet.

My husband's name is Albert. He was born into a sea of Davids, Johns, Stephens, Michaels, and Peters, and he longed to be part of the herd. He toyed briefly with the idea of using the first half of his name and becoming Al, in the hope that everyone would assume he was called Alan, but then he realised that Al Guy didn't really work either. Meanwhile, my mother discouraged me from using any shortened version of my name Patricia which, when combined with a long, unusual surname, made my full name an embarrassing mouthful of noise. After marriage, I rebranded. Pat Guy. Six letters. Tick.

However, sometimes taking your partner's name can present more of a problem than a solution. My friend's mother adored the name Mona and was determined to use it for her first-born daughter. Then she married a Mr Lott, and somehow Mona seemed more edgy than appealing.

I once worked with a lovely headmistress called Penelope who married a Mr Penney. A school friend, one Sue Herring, married a Dave Fish. What are the chances?

Sometimes people's names suit them. Miss Plimsoll, my son's PE teacher. Mrs Hard, the terrifying Music teacher at my primary school. (I subsequently learnt that she was called Miss Izzard.)

As a matter of habit, I always cast an eye down new class lists at the beginning of the school year, automatically registering those names that I assume will be 'ones to watch'. I only realised my subconscious prejudices when my predications were thrown awry by a group of Chinese children with English names: the demeanour and behaviour of Cherry, Roy, Iris, Eric, Jerry, and Vic proving impossible to predict.

I once sat with a rather socially naive judge on a tribunal case involving five siblings whose first names all began with 'Sh'. The judge innocently commented on this unusual situation, wondering aloud if the parents were aware of what they had done. I said I felt sure that it would have been deliberate, but she looked at me doubtfully and continued to muse. 'Shannon, Shyenne, Shardonnay, Sharona … mmm, I can't remember what the baby was called. Was it Shyster?'

Now that would be a name worth living up to. 'And finally, we welcome to the floor, Shyster Smith, the country's new P.M.'

b. <u>Preparing for the birth of a sibling</u>

I have always felt that one of the many excellent features of children's books is that a child can read about any new, exciting, or difficult experience, and see how others have coped: starting school, having a haircut, going to the dentist, staying in hospital, and so on.

When my eldest daughter was expecting her second baby, I thought I would put my money where my mouth was and buy some books for my granddaughter to help her adjust to the imminent arrival of her new sibling. I set off, full of optimism, for my local bookshop.

I selected a few appropriate books and, as one of my granddaughter's favourite characters at the time was Spot the Dog, bought a copy of 'Spot has a New Sister'. To summarise the story: Spot is out playing with his ball in the back garden, his father calls him indoors, says, 'Spot, you have a new sister', opens the door to the under-stairs cupboard and there is Spot's mother, plus Susie the new sister. Sorted. (Thinks – if only it were that simple.)

I looked at the Spot book again when I got home and began to feel a little uneasy. Would this book confuse my granddaughter? Would she develop an all-consuming fear of under-stairs cupboards? Is it perhaps rather odd that we expect young children to happily transfer stories about talking animals that live in houses and go to animal schools, to their own little lives? Would my granddaughter understand the meaning behind the story and relate to it?

Would she have enough common sense to fetch a hammer and nails from the garage and seal up the under-stairs cupboard? 'New baby sister? Oh, I don't think so.'

c. The development of empathy

Empathy is the ability to understand another person's point of view. Children begin to show some understanding of other people's emotions at around two years of age; however, their own feelings will quickly override any empathy if the other person irritates them in some way, perhaps being reluctant to join in with a game, or by playing with a toy that they want.

The best way to teach children empathy is to demonstrate it as an adult, stressing there are always several ways of looking at a situation.

'I'm not that keen on the woman myself, but she means well … She's always lovely to the dog.'

Understanding how others might be feeling will help a child to make allowances. Sometimes people are unkind, because they're embarrassed, frightened, jealous, or upset. When a child realises that their friend is arguing because they're tired or unwell, they may be able to respond more sympathetically.

When siblings argue, sit them down and hold a 'Family Liaison Meeting'. Record the warring factions' areas of disagreement on a large sheet of paper. Each child can offer three points in defence of their behaviour. Provide a conch (see Lord of the Flies). Defendants are not allowed to speak unless they are holding the conch. It will be preferable if the item selected as the conch is made from soft fabric. Divide the time allotted to each child strictly using the second hand of a watch. Discuss each point raised in great detail and to excessive depth. Whenever a fight is threatening to kick off, offer to have a 'Family Liaison Meeting', and soon you will be told, 'Nah, we're good/cool/sorted.' The tedium of the justice system reigns supreme.

d. The importance of good social skills

Children need social skills in order to relate effectively to others. Young children learn social skills from their immediate family through observation and mimicry.

Children's small social circles gradually expand during their early years to include extended family, neighbours, their parent's friends, and adults and children from nursery school and toddler groups. When children start school, they extend their social circle further: peers from their year group, older children, teachers, office staff, the Head teacher, lunchtime supervisors, teaching assistants, and other parents. Different behaviours will be expected from the children when they communicate with these different groups. Teaching children such social conventions is part of the hidden curriculum of all schools.

When children have good social skills, they will be:

- Able to maintain friendships and relationships over time.

- Able to co-operate and compromise, and to 'give and take' with their peers.

- Comfortable in new social situations.

- Able to trust others and to encourage others to trust them.

- Able to problem solve. When social difficulties crop up, the child will stand back and work out what to do, rather than acting impulsively and without thought of possible consequences.

- Able to be assertive when necessary and to apologise when they are in the wrong.

- Positive, happy children who don't complain, or always want to talk about themselves.

e. The development of good social skills

We live in a socially complex world and good social skills are essential for children's happiness. The current generation of children and young people spend a lot of time on social media and, as a result, their ability to relate with others face-to-face may be underdeveloped. Children need to spend time in the real world with real people, as well as speaking to friends on their phones or through social media sites.

Common problems that children experience with social relationships include the following: *(Possible solutions are in italics.)*

A difficulty imagining how other people feel.

✓ *Remember that your child will treat others in the same way that you treat them.*

✓ *Teach your child that all people are important, and always demonstrate consideration towards others yourself.*

✓ *When reading stories with the child, discuss how the characters might be feeling during different parts of the story, to help them to understand the emotions and behaviour of others.*

✓ *Teach children how to express their opinions calmly without being unpleasant or aggressive.*

Being unable to read body language.

✓ *Teach the basics of body language. Help the child to recognise when they are irritating or boring other children; to work out if other children are being friendly or threatening, and if their peers are upset or frightened.*

Finding it hard to apologise.

✓ *Help the child to learn how to repair friendships. Apologising is a useful social skill, but one that doesn't come easily to children; they can find it difficult to admit being in the wrong. When children see adults apologising, they will be more likely to copy the behaviour.*

Having limited friendship groups.

✓ *Encourage the child to make friends in several contexts: school, church, brownies, scouts, sports clubs, youth clubs, and their local neighbourhood. Friendship groups change naturally over time, and the more contacts a child has, the more easily they will adapt to such changes.*

Finding it hard to listen.

✓ *Teach children how to listen actively. Active listeners let the speaker express their point of view without interrupting, disagreeing or challenging. They encourage the speaker by using signs that show they are listening: nodding their head or saying things like mmm, uh-huh, I see. Active listeners will ask questions to show they are interested in the other person and will not turn the conversation round to themselves. They listen to what has been said, rather than wait for their turn to speak. They will respond to the speaker's point, rather than move onto another topic.*

f. Social skills challenges: primary to secondary school transfer

The move from primary to secondary school will be a significant transition in the life of any child. While it is exciting, most children are certain to be apprehensive.

To help the child during this period:

- Practise the journey to school, particularly if it involves public transport or walking/biking along a new route.

- Go through the school checklist together to make sure the child has everything they need.

- Gradually increase your child's independence with practical experiences: going to the local shops on an errand, or walking to a friend's house by themselves.

- Name everything. Lost property is more likely to get back to the child when it is clearly named.

- Photocopy or take a photo of their timetable in case it gets lost.

- Make sure they get to bed in good time, without their phone or any electronic devices.

- Provide them with a water bottle and a healthy snack for the day.

- Show confidence in your child and avoid taking over any tasks that they can do for themselves.

- Welcome old and new friends into your home. The transition between primary and secondary school can be difficult in terms of old and new friendships. Children mature at different ages, and a girl's BFF may suddenly become obsessed with boys and make up, while she is still collecting Sylvanian Family figures. Encourage the children to maintain as wide a circle of friends as possible, to reduce any feelings of guilt or rejection when relationships change.

- Be ready to listen. Be there when your child wants to talk, then if they have a concern or worry later in the year, they will know you are willing to help.

g. Kindness. The roots of kindness.

I recently went to see the re-released musical 'Hair'. I saw the original production in the late '60s, and when my husband suggested going to see the updated play, my initial response was to leave well alone, feeling that some things are best left as a memory. It was therefore, with some reluctance, that I bought him tickets as a birthday present.

I was pleasantly surprised by the production. It was more of a historical observation than cutting-edge theatre, but entertaining, nevertheless. The play focussed on the conflict between the hippy values of the time, and the conscription of American teenagers to fight in the Vietnam War. The action centred around the lifestyle of one specific 'tribe' of hippies, who were constantly banging on about peace, love, and happiness being a desirable way of life for all. However, in one scene the flaw in this ideal could be clearly observed. The girlfriend of the tribe leader purchased him a new shirt. This would appear to have been a thoughtful gift as he had been wearing the same fur waistcoat throughout the first half of the play. The hippy expressed no gratitude, but berated his girlfriend for her small-minded possessiveness, which in turn motivated the unhappy girl to question her boyfriend's high-minded principles. Her musical lament included the lyrics:

'Especially people who care about strangers. Who care about evil and social injustice. Do you only care about the bleeding crowd? How about a needy friend?'

It is very easy to extoll generic virtues in a top down manner, but the transmission of social values is more effective when they are firmly established norms within the child's immediate family group. Adults should demonstrate kindness in family and social circles, thoughtfulness towards older or vulnerable members of the 'tribe' and patience towards younger ones.

h. Kindness. Small acts of kindness.

Human beings are sociable animals: we have always needed to group together in order to survive, and so are programmed to be supportive towards one another.

Being considerate and kind to others will help the child to appreciate the difficulties which some people have to face, put their own problems into perspective, and help them to realise what they have to be happy about.

Example of small ways in which a child could be kind:

1. Letting another child in front of them in the dinner or bus queue.

2. Picking up litter in the playground.

3. Showing polite and considerate behaviour towards adults: neighbours, shop assistants, bus drivers, teachers, school cleaners, and dinner supervisors.

4. Helping a parent lay the table or tidy away after a meal.

5. Letting a sibling watch the TV programme they want without argument.

6. Not joining in if friends tease another child.

7. Volunteering to help with new or younger children at school.

8. Not bearing grudges.

9. Holding doors open for others.

10. Picking up something an adult has dropped.

11. Giving someone a sincere compliment. Telling a classmate that they played a good game of hockey, scored a brilliant goal, or made a fabulous save.

12. Really listening when a friend talks about their worries, and not passing on any confidences.

i. Dealing with bullying

Many children will experience some level of bullying during their school years. Reassure the child that there is nothing wrong with them, the problem is always the bully's, and that they have choices about how to deal with the issue.

✓ <u>Take control of the situation and refuse to be silent</u>. No one should tolerate being bullied. Tell others: your parents, teachers, your form tutor, Head Girl, Head Boy, friends, older children, a Head of Year, prefects, the Librarian, the school nurse, office staff. The problem then become everyone's problem. Bullying often stops as soon as adults and other children find out what's going on, because the bully is afraid that they will be ostracised, punished, or ridiculed.

✓ <u>Be Confident.</u> Bullies lose their power when you don't show fear. Sometimes just acting brave will be enough to stop a bully. Stand tall and speak casually with a confident voice.

✓ <u>Walk away</u>. This puts you in control by removing the bully's opportunity. Bullies want a response, so by behaving as if you haven't noticed them or don't care about them will be the same as not reacting at all.

✓ <u>Stay close to friends.</u> Bullies operate by making their victims feel isolated, so stick close to friends and supportive adults. Walk with friends to school, to lunch, or wherever you think you might meet the bully. Offer to do the same if a friend is having trouble with a bully. Make sure you are always in sight of adults.

✓ <u>Set limits.</u> Don't let the bully get under your skin. Practice your response so you're prepared and can respond quickly without getting upset. Keep it simple and straightforward. If you can't think of anything to say, repeat what they say in a mocking voice, and then walk away.

✓ <u>Be quick and consistent in your response</u>. Bullying usually begins with name-calling or teasing, and how you respond to this will determine whether the bully continues to target you. Bullies like to pick on people who react to taunts, perhaps by getting upset or losing their temper. No response is the best policy. Ignoring the bully and pretending you haven't even registered their presence will put them on the back foot.

✓ <u>Strike while the iron is cold.</u> Sometimes all you have to do with a bully is wait a little while. Think about possible solutions, ask others for their advice, involve adults and other children to help you to find a solution. Always make sure the situation is out in the open for everyone to see.

Why do bullies feel the need to pick on others? Most bullies are trying to make themselves feel more important. Some bullies come from dysfunctional families where everyone is unpleasant, and the child thinks that being aggressive, calling people names, and pushing others around is a normal way to behave. The bully is simply copying what they've seen their family members do. In the end, bullies are side-lined, because other children move on, discover different groups of friends, and leave the bullies behind.

j. Time spent with the extended family

One of the many pleasures of growing older is the increased availability of free time ... or so my children imagine. There is an unspoken assumption that my generation are always available to take care of grandchildren. As a result of the rise in working parents and the cost of quality childcare, many of my peers do spend a significant amount of time providing such support. I have to admit that, although the opportunity to have generous time slots for choosing when and whether to work are a delight, I do enjoy being with this second brood. However, I find myself in a constant state of nervous alert. Will they stop running at the road, fall out of a tree and break an arm, bounce off the bed and knock out teeth? Such hazards seldom occurred to me when raising my own children, but I no longer have the same daily feedback on the developing levels of competence that the children's parents enjoy.

Once I get through the, 'fake it till you make it', stage, I can relax and enjoy the children's company. I am not as rushed as I was when my own family were growing up. I am not doing the school run, hearing each child read the three compulsory pages of their reading book whilst pushing an overloaded buggy with one hand and scrawling comments in the home–school reading record with the other. 'Read with good expression.' 'We really enjoyed this story.' 'What a tedious piece of literature'. I have time to meander along the street, eyes narrowed and focused on the small child ahead, wondering at their behaviour. Why do they post sticks through gates, squat down to observe insects, pick up gravel to sling at passing cars, and ask so many damn fool questions? Happy days.

CHAPTER 2

PERSONAL QUALITIES

INTRODUCTION

What qualities are required for success and happiness in life?

Lewis Terman, an American psychologist, argued that an individual's IQ score would be the strongest predictor of their future success, and in the 1920s Terman started a longitudinal study of 1,500 children identified as having a high IQ. The study continued over the children's lifetime. Ultimately, Terman's study revealed little about the implications of having a high IQ, with the exception of one piece of research carried out by a colleague, Melita Oden. In 1968, Oden compared the hundred most successful and the hundred least successful individuals from Terman's group. (Success was defined as having an occupation that required that person to use their intellectual gifts.) The two groups Oden studied did not differ in IQ scores, but did differ in levels of self-confidence, persistence, and parental encouragement. Oden drew the conclusion that there were other factors that determined an individual's success, above and beyond their intelligence quota.

During the 1970s and 80s, academics began to stress the need for a broader definition of ability.

In 1977, Joseph Renzulli claimed that successful individuals displayed a combination of three types of ability: above-average academic skill, creativity, and task commitment. Renzulli defined 'creative skill' as flexibility, originality, and a willingness to take risks. 'Task commitment' was defined as perseverance, hard work, and fascination with a subject.

In 1983, Howard Gardner suggested several different types of intelligence, including spatial ability, practical aptitude, and social skills.

In 1985, Robert Sternberg described three aspects of ability that define an intelligent person: academic, creative, and practical ability. Practical ability being a talent to apply knowledge in the real world.

1. THE BRAIN AND EDUCATION

a. What do intelligence tests measure?

Historically, intelligence was associated with extraordinary accomplishment: a level of exceptional achievement recognised by other specialists working in the same field.

Alfred Binet, a French psychologist, devised the first intelligence test in the 1900s. Binet's test was designed to identify pupils with special educational needs in order to provide those children with the most appropriate education. The test assessed a child's stage of intellectual development compared to same-aged peers. Binet assumed that children's test results would change over time as a result of their life experience and was opposed to the idea that a child's level of intelligence was fixed, saying, 'We must protest and react against such brutal pessimism.'

However, despite his objections, results from Binet's test were gradually accepted as a permanent marker of an individual's level of intellectual ability.

Towards the end of the 20th century, the assumption that intelligence was an attribute that could be measured by a single test was being regularly challenged, and the belief that an intelligence test measured an individual's ability to complete an intelligence test gained popularity.

b. Who are the gifted and talented?

Schools have traditionally identified two types of intelligent pupils: the gifted and the talented.

- Gifted children perform well across the board. They tend to coast through school, their ability acknowledged by teaching staff; although the children may not always be challenged by or interested in the work they are given.

- Talented children will have outstanding ability in specific areas, for example, Art, Music, Maths, or PE and Dance, but perform at average levels in other subjects.

There are several reasons why the identification of gifted and talented children is not straightforward.

- Ability cannot be spotted without giving a child the opportunity to demonstrate it. Not all schools will have the necessary resources and facilities; for example, a child might not be identified as a talented musician if the school did not have a music department.

- The key factor in identification is the use of as many sources of information as possible. Identification cannot be linked solely to exams and progress tests.

- Blanket screening assessments can be unreliable, and some children may out-think the test if answers appear too obvious.

- Standardised assessments measure a limited range of abilities and require convergent rather than creative thinking. True intelligence isn't what you can do quickly and easily, but how you respond when answers aren't obvious.

- Ability in some areas may not be recognised until Key Stage 3 or 4, when alternative subjects are introduced into the curriculum, and specialist staff generate a new enthusiasm and interest, for example, when ceramics, photography, sculpture, pottery, or print-making are introduced into Art classes.

- Children's development is uneven, and children will vary in their level of maturity. Less than half of the children in the top 5% in Key Stage 2 SATS, will be in the top 5% at GCSE.

- Being labelled as 'able' can damage children's self-confidence when this is associated with easy success. The children may see no-effort academic success as defining their ability and become reluctant to try activities in which they won't succeed immediately.

- Every child is an individual. Children may have assessment scores that are identical, and yet perform in dissimilar ways because of different personality traits, home circumstances, and other factors in their lives.

- Any identification system must spot children with potential, as well as those who are already converting potential into performance. Some able children will be obvious to teaching staff, whereas others who are quieter, less confident, have behaviour problems, or speak English as a second language, may not be so easy to identify. Sometimes intelligent children can exhibit traits that are not popular with the adults in school: they may challenge authority, day-dream, be stubborn, self-opinionated, or weirdly imaginative.

c. Gender and the brain

'Why can't a woman take after a man? Men are so pleasant, so easy to please. Whenever you're with them, you're always at ease. Why can't a woman be like me?' (Professor Higgins. My Fair Lady.)

There are numerous myths surrounding the educational performance of girls.

For example:

1. Girls work conscientiously throughout their time in school, while boys are motivated to work only when deadlines are pending.

There was a general consensus in the Department for Education that GCSEs with coursework favoured girls over boys, as a result of girls' more conscientious approach to study. This was one of the reasons why, when Michael Gove introduced the new GCSEs in 2013, one final exam replaced coursework, thus reducing this female advantage, and presumably shifting the bias in favour of boys. However, in spite of coursework being dropped, GCSE results from 2019 revealed that girls continue to outperform boys across all subjects. 74.3% of girls achieving grade 4 and above, compared to 66% of boys.

2. Girls achieve 'middle of the road' scores in exams, while boys' results cluster around the highest and lowest scores.

In 2019, 5.4% of girls' GCSE grades across all subjects were at the highest level of grade 9, compared to 3.9% of boys' grades. The 2019

'A' Level results reveal that in all subjects, with the exception of Maths and Physics, girls achieved more A*s and As than boys.

There are limited numbers of single-sex state schools, but the Independent School GCSE results for 2019 show that the four schools with the highest GCSE results were girls' schools.

Point = girls are highflyers, not just middle of the road plodders.

What happens between school and work? Do girls over-achieve in school or under-achieve in the workplace? Or could other factors be at play?

- Why are there 428 male MPs, and only 220 female MPs in the House of Commons? (February 2020.)

- Why are there 277 male MPs in the Conservative government and only 87 female MPs? (February 2020.)

- Why, in February 2020, are only 5% of the chief executive officers of the FTSE 100 firms female, when 28% of all leadership roles in these companies are held by women?

- 85% of teachers in primary schools and 62% of teachers in secondary schools are female. Women dominate the teaching profession, but this situation is not reflected in senior management positions, with 72% of primary headteachers and 32% of secondary headteachers being female.

It might be considered demeaning to have artificial gender quotas for influential positions, but the best man for the job (oops, Freudian slip), cannot always be male. Unfortunately, the individuals who are in a position to promote change are those individuals most likely to benefit from maintaining the status quo.

The children's novel, 'Bill's New Frock', by Anne Fine, describes the experience of a young boy who wakes up one morning to find that he has turned into a girl. He is shocked to discover the difference that this change makes to his daily routine. The different way in which he is treated by adults, the behaviour expected from girls, the impractical nature of girls' clothing.

There is a memorable scene in the film, 'Fast Girls', which demonstrates this latter point perfectly. The film is about athletes, specifically a British women's sprint relay team. One night the team go out clubbing, have a disagreement with some men in a bar, and are forced to bolt down the street, chased by the men. The women take off their ridiculously high-heeled shoes, accelerate and sprint away, easily out-pacing their pursuers. Point = women's clothes can be impractical, unsafe, and inhibit females' everyday functioning.

Definition of stag: a strong and proud wild beast. The stag can be differentiated from the rest of the herd by the size of his antlers.

Definition of hen: small, fluffy farmyard bird, makes a lot of noise, unnecessary fussing and lays eggs.

Men's behaviour when gathered as a group can be intimidating, the perfect example being the stag party. Why do men delight in making their BFF, the groom, look ridiculous? Why is it funny to dress the bridegroom as a woman with outsized breasts? Why does the party feel the need to get drunk, fight with each other (plus any other poor soul who gets in their way), and vomit and urinate on street corners?

The aim of women on hen parties is to give their friend, the bride, a pleasant experience sharing events that they hope she will enjoy: a pamper afternoon, shopping, a pleasant meal, or a theatre trip.

Hen and stag events give valuable insights into the extremes of gender behaviour. The majority of women will find it difficult to thrive in a male-dominated environment.

Massive shifts would be required to make changes when stereotypical male/female behaviour is reinforced from birth. Once, at my junior school, a classmate was irritating me, so I thumped him. Truth be told, I expected the one thump would be enough to make him back off, as I always won any fisticuff competition with my older brother, but this boy thumped me back. I gave him another shove, and he gave me one back, and the pushing and shoving quickly developed into a playground fight. The teacher on duty intervened, the boy was matched off to the Head's office for the cane, and I was taken to the First Aid room by my friends. How good was that? I had started the altercation, but all I got was tea and sympathy. Result.

But it really wasn't fair, and very much a 'Bill's New Frock' moment.

d. Multiple intelligences

Howard Gardner's work from the 1980s was seminal in the development of the concept of intelligence. Gardner initially described seven different types of intelligence, adding two further types of intelligence a few years later.

1. <u>Verbal-linguistic intelligence.</u> Children with this type of intelligence enjoy discussions, reading, and writing. They will be confident verbal communicators, who learn well from talks, lectures, and oral presentations.

2. <u>Mathematical-logical intelligence.</u> The ability to reason, calculate, and think in a logical way is an intelligence typically possessed by mathematicians and scientists. Children with this type of intelligence enjoy strategy games, scientific experiments, abstract thought, and the analysis and interpretation of data.

3. <u>Body-kinaesthetic intelligence.</u> The ability to use the body skilfully.

These children will enjoy sport, dance, drama, and design technology. They will learn by doing, enjoy solving problems in practical ways, and prefer to be moving or making, rather than talking.

4. <u>Musical intelligence.</u> These children will enjoy playing instruments, listening and relaxing to music, and going to concerts.

5. <u>Visual-spatial intelligence.</u> Artists, sculptors, painters, and architects all possess visual-spatial intelligence. Children with visual-spatial intelligence have good imaginations, and a strong feel for colour, pattern, and design. They will learn from film, videos, photographs, and diagrams.

6. <u>Interpersonal intelligence.</u> The ability to relate well to others. Children with this intelligence will have good leadership skills, be able to communicate and mediate between groups, and seem to have an instinctive understanding of the feelings and motives of others. They will enjoy working in groups, socialising, and taking part in team activities.

7. <u>Intrapersonal intelligence</u>. Self-knowledge. These children are very aware of their own feelings and motivations. They will be private people, independent, and self-motivated: intuitive day-dreamers who enjoy their own company and like to have time to think and reflect.

The two intelligences that Gardner added later were:

8. <u>Existential Intelligence.</u> This form of philosophical intelligence involves an interest in the meaning of life. Children with this intelligence will have high moral standards and values.

9. <u>Naturalist Intelligence.</u> Naturalist intelligence relates to an appreciation of the natural world. These children will be interested in environmental issues and have an extensive knowledge of nature and the outdoors.

Every individual will have different combinations of these intelligences.

Traditionally, any child who demonstrated verbal-linguistic and/or mathematical-logical intelligence in school would have been considered to be intelligent. Logic and verbal reasoning were seen as superior types of ability. Gardner felt that such assumptions were limited and failed to recognise other abilities and talents that explain why high achievers in schools do not necessarily become high achievers in life.

e. Emotional intelligence

The idea of emotional intelligence was first proposed in the 1990s by American psychologists Peter Salovey, John Mayer, and Daniel Goleman.

Individuals who are emotionally intelligent have a good understanding of their own emotions and the emotions of others and are able to use this knowledge in social interactions.

Goleman developed a framework of five 'elements' that define emotional intelligence:

1. Self-awareness. The individual's ability to recognise their feelings and understand why they might feel the way that they do.

2. Self-regulation. The individual's ability to manage strong emotions such as anger, disappointment, anxiety, and frustration.

3. Empathy. The ability to understand other people's feelings.

4. Motivation. The ability to take action to achieve a goal.

5. Social skill. The ability to communicate and interact appropriately with others.

<u>Children with high levels of emotional intelligence will:</u>

✓ Be popular with others and have a positive effect on other people's sense of well-being.

✓ Be confident and flexible enough to handle uncertainty and change.

✓ Communicate effectively and sensitively with others.

✓ Enjoy strong social relationships and deal successfully with conflicts and disagreements as they arise.

✓ Be able to focus on a future benefit, even when immediate pleasures are appealing. It is difficult to spend the afternoon revising for exams when your friends are all in the park playing football or going to the cinema, but children with good emotional intelligence will have the self-control required to delay immediate gratification.

Most young children will learn such skills incidentally in the home, but Goleman argued that children who do not, can learn emotional intelligence in school.

<u>How to help children to develop emotional intelligence.</u>

o <u>Provide a vocabulary for feelings.</u>

Interpersonal skills will be enhanced when children develop a vocabulary to describe their feelings. 'Upset' being different to 'distraught'. 'Irritated' being different to 'furious'. Explain that strong feelings are part of being human, but even when they are really angry, they should always try to use words rather than actions to deal with the situation.

o <u>Show the child how to manage their emotions.</u>

Helping children to improve their self-regulation is an effective way to develop their emotional intelligence. To understand how to calm themselves down, bounce back from disappointment, deal with frustration and anxiety, and see challenges as opportunities rather than threats.

o <u>Provide lots of opportunities for play.</u>

Giving adequate opportunity for free play will help young children work through their emotions and support the development of empathy.

o <u>Read with the child.</u>

Reading gives children opportunities to explore other people's lives and provides thought-provoking alternative perspectives on life. What is it like to be a refugee, to live on the streets, to be bullied at school, or to have a disability?

o <u>Teach active listening.</u>

Active listening is key to genuine communication and is about more than just paying attention. Active listening involves following another person's conversation, responding to them through sympathetic body language, and demonstrating that you have understood what they said by reiterating their key messages. Active listening will help to promote strong interpersonal relationships.

o <u>Demonstrate empathy towards others as an adult.</u>

Empathy is the ability to appreciate and acknowledge another person's point of view. Children will develop empathy when they receive it themselves.

o Show the child how to consider alternatives.

Teach the children that they have options; to be flexible and always to consider Plan Bs.

'It is a shame that Theo can't come to play today, but his Mummy says that he's too ill to go out. Maybe he can come round at the weekend, and we'll do something else today. We could ring Ruby and see what she is doing, or we could go into town and spend your birthday money. Perhaps Daddy might even take you swimming if we put away the toys in the garden.'

f. Extrovert and introvert

Hubris can be defined as an extreme sense of pride: a dangerous overconfidence combined with arrogance, that is fuelled by a sense of power.

Hubris thrives in situations where extreme self-confidence is confused with competence.

One reason for the rise of privately educated individuals into positions of authority may be the (over) confidence instilled by a private education. Society benefits from drawing from a pool of talent, and there will be limitations in critical thinking, careful analysis, and collaborative problem-solving in public office if all leaders are drawn from a similar background. In the current Cabinet (February 2020), almost 70% of the members attended private schools, with 50% of the Cabinet having gone to either Oxford or Cambridge University.

Over recent decades the Western world has moved towards an increasing fixation on the desirability of 'extrovert' characteristics: assertiveness, verbal ability, and self-assurance. Emphasis is placed in schools on presentation skills, confident public speaking, and quick, decisive thinking. These are the skills possessed by many modern-day politicians, who are self-assured enough to hop from one government department to another, speaking eloquently and confidently about issues of education, transport, defence, health, or housing, with little in-depth knowledge or experience in the field.

Loud, verbally confident individuals tend to be more concerned about their personal image, winning the argument, and defeating the opposition. Viewing others as a threat or a rival may lead to the individual demonstrating diminished levels of considered and co-operative behaviour.

In contrast, as a result of avoiding conflict and public argument, quieter individuals will spend their lives in negotiation and discussion. They will listen to others, be open to compromise, and willing to consider issues from a variety of viewpoints.

Children are all individual and differences in their behaviour need to be taken into account in educational settings. When schools are biased towards the more gregarious and outgoing, the advice given at Parents' Evenings to the parents of quieter children will be to encourage the child to participate more in class, contribute to discussions and try to overcome their 'shyness'. It might benefit society more if teachers were to ask the other parents to try to curb their children's verbosity, to teach them respect for the opinions of others, and to develop a generally more modest attitude in the classroom.

There is no difference in intelligence between the talkative child and the quiet child: they simply behave differently.

Children all have different personalities, and no one personality type is better than any other. Every child needs to feel valued, and able to contribute and participate in their own way.

'If you judge a fish by its ability to climb a tree, it will live its whole life believing that it is stupid.' (Albert Einstein)

g. Bulldozing for the Lord

My second daughter is a popular young woman who has a wide circle of friends. Although she is socially adept, she does enjoy her own company: one of those lucky people who can be the life and soul of a party but does not need to surround herself with others to be happy.

The first school that her eldest daughter attended was a village primary; a school with close links to the local church. My granddaughter asked if she could go to the Sunday School at the church, and my daughter, feeling that the child would enjoy the experience, started to take her to the Sunday Morning Service. A few hymns, verses, prayers, then the children had a bible story and did some colouring in a group at the back of the church, leaving their parents to enjoy a period of reflective peace.

Unfortunately, the vicar head-hunted my daughter and became hell-bent (Freudian slip), on signing her up as an additional Sunday School teacher. My daughter said politely that she could not 'commit to regular attendance', but eventually felt that she was having to be quite rude trying to explain that she simply did not want the job. The vicar would not take no for an answer and collared my daughter and granddaughter one Sunday after Morning Service, telling them to wait in the vestry, while he asked the Sunday School teacher to come and explain what my daughter's new role would involve.

My daughter did not know what else to do but run. She grabbed my bemused granddaughter's hand, legged it round the back of the church and over the graveyard wall. They walked home in silence, my granddaughter's dalliance with religion brought to an abrupt and unnecessary end.

h. The left and right sides of the brain

The traditional view of the neo-cortex or thinking brain was that it consisted of two sides or hemispheres, left and right, with each side having a different function. The right hemisphere would process information in a random, intuitive way, focusing on the overview. The processing carried out by the left hemisphere would be logical and linear and concentrate on the detail.

Traditionally schools have focused on 'left-brain' activities: mathematics and number, language and writing, abstract reasoning, sequencing and analysis. Teachers of older children will tend to adopt a left-brained, linear approach to teaching, working from the part to the whole.

Some psychologists argue that left-brain activities are those preferred by the 'male' brain: an interest in objects rather than people, a need for order and logic, and a tendency towards black and white thinking.

The skills that are possessed by individuals with right-brain dominance have been viewed as being of less academic importance. These attributes would include imagination, intuition, visualisation, and a focus on the bigger picture.

Recent research now shows that this left-brain/right-brain theory is overly simplistic and that, although different areas of the brain do carry out different functions, the definitive performance of each area remain undetermined.

i. Learning styles

Learning styles refer to the different ways in which individuals prefers to learn. Although theories of learning styles are not as popular now as when they were first discussed in the 1980s, the concept continues to raise some interesting questions.

There are numerous Learning Style theories, with probably the most popular being the auditory, visual, and kinaesthetic model.

Auditory learners make up approximately 34% of the population. They will:

- Listen well, enjoy talks and lectures.

- Value discussion and question-and-answer sessions.

- Learn through reading.

- Be good with words and enjoy challenging wordy problems.

Visual learners make up 29% of the population. They will:

- Be creative and imaginative day-dreamers.

- Appreciate being given the overview of a topic to help with their understanding.

- Draw and doodle as they listen.

- Prefer to learn using visual images (films, videos, or YouTube clips), rather than written text or auditory instructions.

- Find prolonged periods of listening difficult, because they are distracted by visual stimuli: a car passing the window, the teacher's new shoes, or a spider crossing the ceiling.

<u>Kinaesthetic learners make up 37% of the population. They will:</u>

- Enjoy physical activity.

- Move about a lot, fidget, and be easily distracted.

- Be good at practical subjects: Sport, Design Technology, Dance, and Drama.

- Have high levels of energy.

- Learn by doing.

- Work in short bursts.

- Appreciate the use of practical apparatus and resources, field trips, and visits to relevant places of interest.

Most children are able to use different ways of learning in different situations, but some children will have a marked preference for one style of learning. Problems may arise if a child has one dominant learning style but is taught by a teacher who uses another style for teaching. This goes some way to explaining the situation where a child blossoms in one teacher's class but performs badly the following year in a different teacher's group.

Many teachers, particularly in secondary schools, have an auditory teaching style. They feel most comfortable passing information on to the children verbally. This will seem to them to be the most effective way to get information across, particularly when the curriculum is content heavy and time is tight. Practical activities: project work, videos, experiments, field trips, interactive games, class discussion and independent research may seem like optional, fun activities, rather than valid ways of learning.

The formal teaching approaches prevalent in secondary schools will be a move away from the more multi-sensory teaching of KS2. Practical activities and 'learning by doing', being a feature of the primary curriculum.

However, many secondary school children continue to need a 'hands on' approach to their learning.

A few years ago, I trialled a Learning Style Questionnaire with a Year 11 bottom Maths Set in the school where I was working. The results for the fifteen children in this set showed that they all had a kinaesthetic/practical learning preference. Was this just coincidence? Are all kinaesthetic learners poor at Maths? Or was Maths being taught in a way that didn't suit these children's learning style and gradually, over time, they had all drifted down into the bottom set?

Kinaesthetic learners can be overlooked in secondary school. This may be because there is an assumption that intelligence is linked to mental, rather than practical, aptitude. The unspoken hierarchy that exists in schools has always defined certain subjects to be of more value than others. Maths, Sciences, and Languages feature at the top of the academic tree, Humanities in the middle, with Music and Visual Arts ranked slightly below, but above Drama, DT and Dance. Sport and Games appearing as optional extras. This unspoken bias may make teachers feel they should teach pupils in abstract, formal ways in order to develop their intellect, thereby excluding the 'hands on' learner.

j. A 'Learning Style' questionnaire

This questionnaire can be used to get a better understanding of your learning preferences.

Give yourself a mark out of five for each statement. A score of five would mean that there is a strong correlation between the statement and the way you like to work. 0 would be when there is no match whatsoever. If you agree with the statement sometimes, give yourself a score between 1 and 4 depending on the frequency of the match.

SECTION A

- ➢ In activities that involve a lot of listening, I lose concentration easily.
- ➢ I find instructions difficult to recall when they are given verbally.
- ➢ When learning about something new, I prefer to watch a video, rather than listen to a speaker.
- ➢ I watch and think during lessons, rather than talk and act.
- ➢ I find it difficult to remember jokes.
- ➢ I would rather be shown how to do something, than be told how to do it.
- ➢ I doodle during lessons.
- ➢ I have a general difficulty with concentration.
- ➢ My handwriting is clear and neat.
- ➢ I understand and memorise information more effectively, when I am able to see it in diagram, map, or graphic form.

TOTAL POINTS =

SECTION B

- ➢ I find it difficult to sit still.
- ➢ I fidget and move about more than my friends.
- ➢ I enjoy making things.

- I use my hands to emphasise points and appear animated when talking.
- I dress for comfort, with a preference for casual rather than formal clothes.
- I am a weak speller.
- I prefer games with action and noise, rather than quiet games like chess.
- I often refer to things as 'whatsits' or 'thingamajigs'.
- I solve problems by working them through in a practical way.
- I feel irritated if I have to sit and listen for long periods.

TOTAL POINTS =

SECTION C

- I enjoy talking and discussion.
- I find it easy to remember instructions.
- I prefer to listen to music, rather than view art or design.
- I am easily distracted by noise and appreciate a quiet environment for working.
- I enjoy crosswords and other wordy puzzles and games.
- I like group work.
- I remember things that I have heard, rather than things that I have seen.
- I enjoy listening to the radio.
- I like riddles and puns.
- I often hum and sing to myself.

TOTAL POINTS =

Section A = A visual learning bias. Total score =

Section B = A kinaesthetic learning bias. Total score =

Section C = An auditory learning bias. Total score =

k. How auditory, visual, and kinaesthetic learners can maximise their learning

34% of children are auditory learners. The following activities will suit their learning style:

✓ Listening to talks and presentations.

✓ Reading around the topic.

✓ Going to the theatre to hear set English texts presented in different ways.

✓ Group work, class discussion, and summarising information with others.

✓ Reading work aloud.

✓ Acting out set texts to focus on the language the author is using.

✓ Explaining the subject to another person.

29% of children will have a visual learning preference. The following activities will suit their learning preference:

✓ Creating mind maps, charts, diagrams, or information timelines.

✓ Watching videos, films, and YouTube clips.

✓ Using interactive computer sites.

✓ Using illustrated books with charts, graphs, cartoons, and diagrams to help with the understanding of a topic.

✓ Recording key facts, perhaps by making colourful notes that incorporate sketches, illustrations, or computer graphics.

✓ Studying photos and pictures.

37% of children are kinaesthetic learners. The following activities will suit their learning preference:

✓ Learning through practical activities, games, and demonstrations.

✓ Acting out scenes from set texts.

✓ Role play.

✓ Working in short, concentrated bursts, with regular movement breaks.

✓ Going on field trips and school visits.

✓ Carrying out research on internet sites.

✓ Word processing notes in different colours, fonts, or print to make them visually attractive. Using highlighting, italics, or underlining in notes to draw attention to dates, names, or key terms.

1. How the brain learns

It is useful for all children to understand how to get the most from their brain.

➤ The brain appreciates the repetition of information. The more frequently information is revisited, the better the recall of that information will be. Hence the need to revise before tests and exams.

➤ The brain works by making connections. In order to make sense of information, the brain will try to link new information with the children's existing knowledge. The more related information the brain is exposed to, the more links it can make, and the more secure the learning. The child could read magazine and newspaper articles, watch films and DVDs, or visit places of interest that relate to the topic they are studying.

> The brain enjoys variety. The unusual (funny, rude, ridiculous) will be more memorable than the mundane.

> The brain learns actively. The brain works best when it has to think about, and do something with information, for example: changing wordy text into a diagram, graph, chart, or timeline, and discussing or explaining information to others.

> The brain needs to be focussed. The child must pay attention if they want to learn.

> Brain health and physical health are closely linked. When children are distracted, tired, uncomfortable, thirsty, or hungry, they will not learn.

> The brain requires adequate nourishment. The brain uses 20% of the body's food intake and will perform less efficiently when its energy supply drops.

> The brain needs a good supply of oxygen. When the child exercises regularly, the brain will receive enough oxygenated blood to function effectively. Just standing up increases the blood supply to the brain by 15%.

> Stress has an impact on brain function. The brain can be divided into three sections: the reptilian brain, the mammalian brain, and the neocortex. The primitive, or reptilian brain, is responsible for the fight-or-flight response, the mammalian brain controls emotions, and the neocortex is involved in intellectual thought. When a child is anxious or afraid, the reptilian brain will take over

and divert all energy to the limbs to prepare the individual to run or stay and fight. The brain's neocortex, or thinking brain, will be unable to function when the reptilian brain is activated.

➤ <u>Adequate sleep is essential for good brain function</u>. Sleep is the time when the brain is able to order and organise recent events and create long-term memories.

m. The brain and nutrition

The brain makes up 2% of our body weight but uses 20% of our food intake.

The most beneficial diet for the brain is the 'Mediterranean' diet. The fresh fruit and vegetables in this diet will supply all of the vitamins that the brain requires.

1. Nuts and seeds contain high levels of <u>vitamin E,</u> beneficial for overall brain health.

2. <u>Vitamin C</u> improves mental agility by strengthening the brain's neurotransmitters. Vitamin C can be found in: blueberries, broccoli, tomatoes, pineapples, peas, and blackcurrants.

3. Leafy vegetables contain <u>vitamin K</u> to boost brain cell growth.

4. <u>Omega-3 fatty acids</u> help communication between nerve cells in the brain. These fatty acids can be found in oily fish, such as salmon, sardines, and tuna, pumpkin seeds, and walnuts.

5. <u>Iron</u> is used to transport oxygen in the red blood cells to the brain. The brain uses 25% of the body's oxygen intake. Iron is found in meat, dried fruit, and green vegetables.

6. Eggs and milk contain <u>vitamin B.</u> Vitamin B maintains memory function, and assists in the production of red blood cells. (See point 5.)

7. An adequate amount of <u>water</u> is essential as the brain is made up of 70% water.

The brain requires a regular supply of nutrients, so ensure the children have a good breakfast and do not skip meals.

2. EXECUTIVE FUNCTIONING SKILLS

a. What is Executive Functioning?

Executive functioning describes the management system of the brain. A comparison can be drawn between executive functioning and the conductor of an orchestra. A conductor will co-ordinate the different sections of the orchestra, bringing in the brass section, whilst holding back the percussion, but maintaining the string section's input quietly in the background. A child's executive functioning will act in the same way to regulate input from the different areas of their brain. 'I must pay attention now, keep my memory ready, but don't need to plan my response yet.'

Executive functioning does not fully develop until the individual is in their mid-twenties. This slow maturity of the brain's control system goes some way to explain the sometimes impulsive and apparently irresponsible behaviour of teenagers.

One of the most popular models of executive functioning describes six aspects of the system: action, activation, effort, emotion, focus, and memory.

- <u>Action</u> refers to the child's ability to track and evaluate their performance; to monitor the success of their strategies and adapt their approach accordingly.

- The <u>activation</u> aspect of executive functioning refers to the child's ability to motivate themselves to work, to accurately estimate the amount of time required for a task, to plan and organise their approach, and complete the work to a satisfactory standard.

- The <u>effort</u> aspect relates to the child's ability to sustain consistent effort and appropriate work-rate over time.

- The <u>emotion</u> aspect of executive functioning refers to the child's ability to manage their feelings, control their emotions, think before acting, and anticipate the consequences of their behaviour.

- <u>Focus</u> refers to the child's ability to maintain concentration and avoid distractions whilst working.

- There are several types of <u>memory</u>, but the one that is most important for children in school is working memory. Working memory requires the child to recall information from memory, and then to use that information while completing other tasks.

<u>Illustrative example</u>: Nine-year-old Amy has been diagnosed with dyslexia. Amy has excellent verbal skills, is imaginative and creative, but has comparatively low levels of literacy, a weak working memory and poor co-ordination. Amy constantly loses personal possessions and produces disorganised and untidy written work. She has limited interest in topics that hold no intrinsic appeal and finds it hard to concentrate in some lessons. Although poorly co-ordinated, Amy excels in movement, drama, and IT. As a result of her verbal ability and social skill, she is able to play the class clown with devastating effect.

<u>Strategies to support Amy's executive functioning could include:</u>

1. <u>Action</u>. Amy has excellent verbal skills and enjoys discussion with older children and adults, therefore a mentoring system that

focuses on developing her metacognitive skills and self-advocacy would be beneficial.

(Metacognition = learning how to learn. Self-advocacy = speaking up for yourself.)

2. Activation. Whole class discussion and input on suitable techniques for planning and organising work, with IT used to support Amy's personal organisation and time management.

3. Effort. Amy is highly motivated when she finds a task interesting, so see if there is an aspect of the work that appeals to her. Break tasks down into small steps and provide regular feedback to maintain her impetus. Personal challenges will interest and motivate her, perhaps using a timer to extend her period of concentration.

4. Emotion. Amy would benefit from recognition and praise for any display of mature and thoughtful behaviour, and perhaps an appointment to a position of responsibility to show an appreciation of her personal and social skill. Use IT to enable Amy to take a pride in the production of well-presented pieces of work that reflect her creative potential.

5. Focus. Active teaching techniques will help to meet Amy's need for a comparatively higher level of stimulation: class discussions, computer work, interactive games, and the use of drama and role play. Regular breaks where Amy is allowed to move around the classroom: giving out books, opening the windows or collecting in homework, will provide opportunities for legitimate physical movement.

6. Memory. Use IT, practical apparatus and resources to reduce the load on Amy's working memory. Draw links between remembering lines in Drama or complicated dance routines and the recall of information in class.

b. An Executive Functioning Questionnaire

Questionnaires provide a useful starting point to explore and discuss executive functioning.

A questionnaire to explore aspects of the child's executive functioning and raise issues for discussion.

Action: an individual's ability to monitor and regulate their actions

- What sort of lessons do you enjoy or find interesting, and why?

- In which subjects do you make most effort and why?

- Do you work well with others, or do you prefer to work alone? Are you happy to do both?

- Are there any specific aspects of learning you would like help with, for example: planning essays, learning German vocabulary, revising for tests, or the correct use of punctuation?

- Can you work out ways to improve your performance?

Activation: organising tasks and materials, time management

- What are your targets for the coming year in school?

- How well do you organise yourself? Would you say you were well organised?

- Are you able to keep on top of your workload?

- Do you always complete homework on time?

- Do you know how to plan essays, projects, and revision?

- Do you ever find it difficult to get started on work? Do you ever leave work until the last minute?

Effort: staying alert and sustaining motivation

- What motivates you to work hard?

- Do you find it hard to stay alert?

- When are you alert? When are you lethargic? Are there any patterns to this?

- What do you do to help yourself to stay alert?

- Do you have any problems with sleeping?

Emotion: managing frustration and modulating feelings

- Would you say that you are an emotional person?

- Do you lose your temper or get upset easily? If so, when/why?

- What makes you happy in school?

- What do you enjoy outside school?

- What makes you unhappy in school?

Focus: finding, sustaining, and shifting attention as required. Controlling impulse behaviour

- Do you ever get told off for not listening?

- Can you concentrate on homework for the required period of time? What might distract you? How do you try to recover your focus?

- Do you ever speak before thinking?

- Do you find it hard to sit still for any length of time?

- Can you adapt plans and take unexpected events in your stride?

Memory: using working memory and accessing recall.

- Do you ever feel that your memory lets you down?

- Do you find it easy to learn French/German/Spanish vocabulary?

- Did you learn your number bonds/times tables easily?

- Do you remember things you have to do without being reminded?

c. Executive functioning: hot and cool skills

The executive functions of the brain can be divided into two groups: hot and cool skills.

1. Hot executive functioning relates to the regulation of emotion. How well does the child manage their emotions? They might want to lash out at another child in the heat of the moment but manage to curb the impulse and walk away. Some children will have significant difficulty controlling their reaction to frustration, anxiety, anger, or irritation. This may appear to adults to be a behavioural problem.

2. Cool skills refer to those executive functioning skills that do not involve emotions; such skills as organisation, time management, or memory.

Emotion say hurry. Wisdom says wait.

Tantrums in younger children because of an immaturity of executive functioning are common. Tantrums may morph into impulsive behaviour in older children and teenagers. As executive functioning skills do not fully mature until the individual is in their mid-twenties, many teenagers will make poor decisions that they later regret. When other factors are added, such as hormonal changes and peer pressure, it is easy to understand why some teenagers choose to drink and drive, to dive into river water of an unknown depth, or mess about on railway lines; even when their cool executive skills are telling them that these are dangerous things to do.

Most children learn with maturity, to control their impulsive, knee jerk, 'hot' reactions, and to engage the thinking brain, or 'cold' executive functioning.

d. Self-regulation

Self-regulation is an aspect of hot executive functioning and describes the individual's ability to manage their behaviour: regulating their emotions when excited or angry, controlling impulsive responses, and calming themselves down when irritated or anxious.

Self-regulation correlates closely to success in life. Children with good levels of self-regulation will grow into adults who think before acting and make better decisions: not to eat that extra slice of cake, not to buy something they cannot afford, and to resist the temptation to tell the boss what they really think.

The ability to self-regulate will enable the child to behave in a socially acceptable way: to share, take turns, negotiate with others, compromise, and empathise with peers.

Self-control develops gradually from early childhood. Toddlers will have tantrums and may hit or bite another child when overwhelmed by their emotions. By the time a child starts school, they will have a better understanding of other people's feelings and appreciate that situations can be viewed from several angles.

There will always be differences between individual's levels of self-control: emotional children will find it harder to self-regulate than children who are easy-going.

Helping children to develop self-regulation

- Children develop self-regulation by enjoying warm and responsive relationships with others, and by watching the adults around them demonstrate calm, considerate, and thoughtful behaviour.

- Help your child find appropriate ways to deal with strong emotions before any hot feelings take over. To try to halt their anger by using the thinking, logical part of the brain. Is this irritating person really important? Do I really care what they think? Will this matter so much tomorrow/by the weekend/next week?

- Show the child how to distract themselves mentally from challenging situations. To try to remember all the characters from Harry Potter books, to say the months of the year backwards, or remember everything they did yesterday from the moment they got up.

- Be patient with the child. Keep repeating the same reassuring responses.

- Give the child a warning when you anticipate they might find it hard to deal with a situation.

  'When Clare and baby Reuben come over this afternoon, you'll need to shut the door to your bedroom in case Reuben wants to play with your Scalextric.'

- As an adult, acknowledge the child's emotions, then provide alternative ways of coping: 'Did you throw the car away because you were cross when it didn't work? Next time, ask me, and we can mend it together.'

- Model self-control.

  'I find it really hard to paint neatly, but if I paint a few bits at a time, I'll be able do it properly without making mistakes and getting cross with myself.'

- Praise your child when they show self-control. 'You were kind to let Theo go first on the swing.'

- Match your expectations to the child's age and stage of development. This will help the child avoid the frustration of not being physically, intellectually, or emotionally mature enough to comply with whatever they are being asked to do.

- Remember that many things can affect a child's ability to self-regulate: being tired, ill, hungry, frightened, excited, or anxious will all have an impact on the child's self-control.

e. Delayed gratification

'Delayed gratification' refers to those situations where an individual is able to defer an immediate reward for some long-term gain.

For example:

- The child could watch TV the night before an exam or revise for the exam in the hope of a better grade.

- Learning a new skill, for example, how to play the drums, will require the child to give up some free time, but will enable him/her to join the school band.

A child's ability to delay gratification is an important aspect of self-regulation. Research indicates that an individual's ability to delay gratification leads to increased academic and working life success.

3. RESILIENCE

a. What are Growth and Fixed Mindsets?

Carol Dweck, a psychologist from Stanford University, argues that some children feel their potential is pre-determined, and that nothing they can do will change this. They feel that they were born with limited ability in Maths, for example, in the same way that they were born with blue eyes and auburn hair. The child believes that everyone is born somewhere on a spectrum running from clever and talented, to less able and unintelligent, and that their position on this line is impossible to change. Dweck refers to this way of thinking as having 'a fixed mindset'.

Other children will feel able to increase their levels of skill through effort and perseverance. Dweck refers to this way of thinking as possessing a 'growth mindset'.

Dweck estimates that 40% of the population have a fixed mindset and 40% a growth mindset. The other 20% vary between the two options; perhaps understanding that if they practise more, their skateboarding would improve, but feeling that German will always be beyond them.

Dweck maintains that fixed mindsets are encouraged in school because of a narrow focus on academic achievement.

Fixed Mindsets

In school, successful children with a fixed mindset will try to protect their reputation of intelligence and be threatened by other children's ability. Satisfaction will come from doing better than their peers. When pupils see other children as competition, their enthusiasm for co-operative problem solving will be limited.

Some of these children may worry that they are not as bright as people think, and be afraid of tackling challenging work, experimentation, or collaboration with others in case they fail.

They will deny having done revision for tests. They may coast through exams (because of their 'innate' ability), or crash (because they 'didn't bother revising'). Children with fixed mindsets tend to plateau early and underachieve.

Other children with fixed mindsets who see themselves as failures in school will assume that they were born stupid and are powerless to change their position. They will be disheartened when faced with something they do not understand immediately or work that they feel is beyond them. They will see co-operation with others or working things out slowly as evidence of their lack of ability. They may prefer to cheat rather than be seen to struggle. Some of these pupils will withdraw and complain that school is 'boring'. Others will channel their frustration into sabotaging situations that make them feel uncomfortable, creating problems for teachers and other children.

Growth Mindset

Children with a growth mindset believe their ability will improve if they work hard and keep trying. They will feel able to make things happen, be motivated to learn, and continue to extend their achievement.

These children will say:

- 'I can get better at French if I learn more vocabulary.'
- 'I can't understand this yet. I'll go to Maths Surgery at lunch time and see if Mrs Boxford can explain it to me again.'
- 'I started learning German after everyone else. I'll have to work twice as hard to catch them up.'

To develop a Growth Mindset in children:

✓ Be aware of the language used to praise children. Try to avoid saying things such as: 'You'll find this very easy, because you're so good at this sort of thing.'

✓ Encourage friendships with positive, enthusiastic people. A 'can do' attitude will rub off on children.

✓ Help the child to be flexible in their thinking. There are lots of ways to tackle problems, to deal with challenges, and overcome obstacles. Encourage them to think of approaches that complement their way of working.

✓ Celebrate effort as well as talent.

✓ When a child succeeds at a task, encourage them to think about why they were successful, and then use that understanding in the future.

✓ Help the child to focus on a purpose or end result and not to give up.

'I want to swim for the 'A' Team and get school colours. I'll keep going to training to work on my upper body strength. I know I can improve.'

b. Resilience

Resilience is taken from the Latin word 'resiliant' meaning to rebound. Resilience is the term used to describe an individual's ability to bounce back from disappointment. Psychologists have identified common characteristics found in the resilient individual. These characteristics include: an ability to problem solve, a sense of humour, positive self-esteem, good social skills, and optimism. Everyone will be frustrated by life at some time, but it is the ability to be disappointed and then move on, that is the mark of the resilient individual.

Children can be taught how to be more resilient.

- Encourage the child to accept what has happened, emphasising that ruminating on a situation will change nothing. Feel the disappointment, acknowledge it, but do not dwell on it. The sooner the child can leave regrets behind, the sooner they will be able to carry on as normal.

- Teach the child to use distraction techniques to avoid negative over thinking: run around the block, go for a bike ride, read a book, go out with friends, get involved in a favourite hobby.

- Encourage the child to plan ahead, be optimistic about their ability to solve problems and to believe that they will succeed in the future.

  'If I had scored more goals in practice, I'm sure I would have been selected for the team. I'm disappointed, but I'll keep going to lunchtime training, and see if Dad will practise taking penalties with me on Saturday morning.'

- Resilient individuals will accept that frustrating things happen to everyone but won't take failure personally. They understand that they are responsible for what they gain from an experience; to learn the lesson, make the necessary changes and then move on.

  'I could have done better in the test, if I hadn't had to cram at the last minute. I'll space revision out over a couple of nights for the next test.'

- Help the child to develop the competences they require. For example, when they are sitting school exams, to decide how they revise best, or to experiment with a few new ways of revising.

- Encourage the child to always have a Plan B.

  'If it rains on my birthday, and we can't play football in the park. We can come back home and watch a match on television.'

- Help the children to think flexibly. When they find themself in a challenging situation, encourage them to alter their perspective as the situation unfolds and not to get stuck trying to follow one single solution.

- Remind them of fans of sports teams. They know that sometimes their team will lose or perform badly. They won't win the Cup or move up a league every season, but they will always have another chance in the future.

c. Grit

When a child is described as having 'grit', they will have demonstrated an ability to keep going through adversity and persevere as they work towards long-term goals.

In Malcom Gladwell's book 'Outliers', he discusses the '10,000-Hour Rule.' Gladwell claims that all successful individuals display an impressive ability to persevere. Gladwell estimates that a least 10,000 hours of practice are required to become successful in a specific field. He uses the example of The Beatles' experience of playing live in Germany between 1960 and 1964, before they became international stars. Gladwell calculates that appearing on stage for over 10,000 hours during that period enabled the group to perfect their performance.

Another underlying condition for grit is what psychologists call 'passion'. Passion is the term used to describe an individual's overwhelming enthusiasm for what they like to spend time doing. Many children on the ASC spectrum have high levels of grit, because of what might be called their 'obsessive' interests: these obsessive interests could be seen as passions.

4. CREATIVITY

a. Encouraging children to think creatively

Creativity is the ability to imagine or to make something that hasn't existed previously. Creative thinkers will find novel or unorthodox solutions to problems; solutions that are not dependent upon past or current thinking. In a rapidly changing world, this type of innovative thinking is essential if society is to evolve successfully.

'It is not the strongest of the species that survive, nor the most intelligent, but the most responsive to change.' (Charles Darwin. Scientist.)

Professor George Land started a study into creativity in the U.S. in the 1960s. Land carried out creativity assessments on children in the three-to-five-years age group. He tested the same children at 10 years of age, and then again at 15 years of age. While the assessments identified the degree of creativity in five-year olds at 98%, their levels had dropped to 30% by the age of 10, and then dropped further to 12% at 15 years of age. When the same test was given to 280,000 adults, Land found their creativity levels to be at a 2% level. Current education systems cannot be relied upon to teach children to think creatively: but seem to be more likely to teach pupils to follow instructions and adhere to routine behaviour.

What hinders creative thinking:

o Habit. Individuals get used to doing something in a certain way and find it hard to break the habit.

o Fear of change. Many individuals prefer to stay in familiar situations and so will avoid making changes.

o Fear of making mistakes. Being afraid of making errors and appearing foolish in front of others.

o Self-doubt. 'What makes me think I would know better than anyone else? No one will take my ideas seriously'.

o Lack of time. 'I simply do not have enough time to think about this, or to consider any alternatives.'

o Fear of seeming childish. 'Will my idea seem silly or overly simplistic to professional colleagues?'

o Fear of consequences. 'What if I get this wrong and the consequences of my mistake are serious?'

b. Top tips for creative thinking

To be creative children need to:

Play. One of the most important forms of creative training for children is play: rough and tumble play, construction play, imaginative play, social play, and physical play. Nothing reinforces children's creativity more than engaging in free play for regular periods of time throughout the day.

Have a degree of competency in, and knowledge of, a relevant area. Creativity is based on understanding and knowledge, so a child must have some level of competency in the area before they are able to think creatively. The more they know about a topic, the more creative they can be in their thinking. When children have limited experience and knowledge, they will revert to tried and tested ways of working, functioning well in routine activity, but finding it harder when originality is required. It is important that children are encouraged to learn new things and to follow new interests, even if their enthusiasm is short lived.

<u>Practise thinking creatively</u>. Children need to practise 'thinking outside of the box' on a regular basis or they will default to usual thinking patterns. Creative thinking practice in informal situations will build their confidence. Simple warm-ups could include the, 'How many ways can you use a paperclip', type of activity. For paperclip, substitute a piece of string, key, pencil, or bucket, and then allow the child two minutes to compile a list of possible uses.

Lateral thinking puzzles are also useful to break entrenched patterns of thinking. Books containing such puzzles can be bought at most stationery and book shops, or on-line.

<u>Be able to generate numerous ideas</u>. More ideas will mean more possibilities to consider. Encourage children's interest in different areas to create new mixes of ideas: to link experience gained from playing hockey, with scientific facts, in order to solve a problem in Geography. Most new ideas are a mix of old ideas assembled in a different way; new recipes based on old recipes, alternative ways of cooking a dish, new ingredients that could be added, or different sides that could be served with the dish.

<u>Consider extreme ideas</u>. Considering extreme ideas might appear unnecessary, but links may be made between different parts of unusual ideas to make them worthwhile.

<u>Read</u>. Reading is one of the best ways to promote creativity. The

child will need to use their imagination whilst reading to conjure up images to accompany stories. Make up stories with your child or discuss alternative endings for the story you are reading. Fiction CDs serve the same purpose as reading a book, but TV programmes or videos do not. TV images are already on the screen, and the child does not have to imagine the characters or their setting.

Be brave. A fear of looking foolish will limit some children's creative thinking. When the child realises that everyone makes mistakes, they will feel able to take more risks. Even the most eminent scientists will go down a lot of blind alleys before making significant discoveries. Mistakes teach necessary lessons and help the individual to find better ways of working.

Work collaboratively and consider other people's point of view. A child's idea may work for them, but what will it look like from their friend's or a sibling's point of view? Creativity is often sparked by being with others who hold different views, or by imagining what other people's ideas might be. Might another child have some alternative experience or additional knowledge that could be useful?

Daydream. Children will have their best ideas when their brains are relaxed. Novel and innovative ideas cannot be rushed but require a period of incubation if they are to be clarified and improved. Stressful, constant engagement will not give a child enough time to think creatively. It may be hard for an adult to sit in the car without turning the radio on, travel on the train or wait at a bus stop without reaching for their mobile, but by constantly seeking out external ways to amuse ourselves, we are teaching children to ignore their surroundings; the natural world, other people, and simple, slow-moving pleasures.

A child may think about a problem all day, then get their best idea when they stop considering the problem, relax and let their mind drift, perhaps while walking the dog, having a bath, or (irritatingly), in the middle of the night when half asleep. The brain is particularly good at making links and connections while the individual sleeps.

Children need time to be alone with their thoughts, to process information, to allow the brain to re-run scenarios and consider alternative solutions to tasks or situations.

Participate in art and craft activities. Art and craft activities encourage creative expression, which in turn will nurture the imagination. Unfortunately, in many schools, the creative curriculum has been reduced in order to ensure there is enough time to cover the academic curriculum.

Be curious. Without curiosity, children will be passive learners and accept whatever they are told without question. Encourage the child to keep an open mind. Model curiosity yourself by wondering aloud about information. If the child asks you a question, research the answer with them. The more curious the child is, the more creative they will be.

c. Divergent and convergent thinking

Divergent thinking describes the ways individuals think when they want to produce a lot of ideas covering as many different options as possible. Divergent thinking is at the heart of creativity.

Convergent thinking describes the situation where the individual chooses the best idea from a few options. Usually this involves giving the correct answer to a closed question.

Often in schools, children will be presented with the one correct answer to a question, and their work marked against this. However, in real life there is rarely one perfect solution to a problem.

Creative thinking to music

One of the more obtuse and yet useful advantages of the internet is the opportunity to research song lyrics. This never used to be an option and confusion over lyrics was rife. One of my school friends always felt that the Beach Boys must be a gay band because they went to a dance looking 'for a man', when there were actually there looking 'for romance'. (Barbara Ann. 1965.) Most people can link significant events from their youth to songs of the time. Who they were friends with, who they were going out with, and where they were when they first heard the track.

Some songs are memorable because they are so irritating. I was put off many singles after dire Pan's People performances on Top of the Pops. (Pan's People being the show's in-house dance group.) 'Someone's knocking on the door' ('Let 'Em In'. Wings. 1976.) being a prime example. The performance involved Pan's People skipping around a collection of four cardboard doors and knocking on them all in turn. Imaginative stuff.

The woman in Roy Orbison's 'Pretty Woman' video of 1964 was wearing a particularly bad pair of shoes, and I disliked the song by association.

However, lyrics burn into your brain and over the years I have acquired a habit of finishing off a verse or chorus if someone unintentionally starts the first line:

Them: 'Oh well. It's now or never.'

Me: 'Come hold me tight. Kiss me, my darling, be mine tonight.'

Such a conversation would not cause a problem among peers of the same age but is more difficult when the other person has no idea of the link you are making, and hazards a guess at your motives. You explain the lyrics are taken from an Elvis Presley track of 1960, adding quickly that you only know the words because your Mother bought all of Elvis's records as a child, kept her collection, and played them to you decades later as lullabies.

Misunderstandings can also occur with pupils. When children are hanging about my classroom, not wanting to head off to Physics, Hockey, or some other unattractive option, but preferring to stay and chat, I will say:

'Right, just go ...' pause '... walk out that door, just turn around now, 'cause you're not welcome any more'.

By the time I get to the line, 'Weren't you the one who tried to hurt me with goodbye. Do you think I'd crumble? ...' they have all bolted.

Once, concerned such a conversation might be followed up by the school's Child Protection mafia, I explained to the pupils that these particular words were taken from the lyrics of the Gloria Gaynor classic, 'I Will Survive', and therefore a song they would all be familiar with. They claimed not to have heard of Gloria Gaynor, let alone the song, and looked her up on their phones. Turns out the record was released in 1978 and they were all born in 2005.

Me: 'What? Are you certain? Let me look at that.'

I now try to be more careful to ensure that no one can work out the exact tracks of my years (The Tracks of my Tears. The Miracles. 1965), but recently I went to my grandson's Harvest Festival Celebration, and the occasion set biblical poetry in motion (Poetry in Motion. Bobby Vee. 1961.)

Them: 'The wind's cold today.'

Me: 'Ah, the cold wind in the winter, the pleasant summer sun, the ripe fruit in the garden ...' (All Things Bright and Beautiful. Cecil Alexander. 1884.)

5. COURAGE

a. Courage. Encouraging children to be brave.

Being courageous involves doing something in spite of being afraid. Adults never regret what they have done, only what they haven't; and children should not confuse fear that keeps them safe, with fear that stops them from doing what they want to do.

To help children to be brave:

- Encourage the child to try to do something courageous every day. This might be putting their hand up to answer one question in every lesson, joining the school choir, going to a friend's house for tea, climbing a tree in the park, or speaking to a neighbour. It doesn't have to be anything huge, just something they would normally shy away from. Once they have decided what they are going to do, encourage them to just do it without over thinking, so they do not have time to change their mind.

- Teach children to focus on what they can do and what they have already done, rather than what they feel they can't do and haven't done. To think positively about the benefits of being brave, remember a previous success, and give it a go.

- Encourage the child to be flexible, open minded, and adventurous and to cultivate a 'nothing ventured, nothing gained' attitude.

- Demonstrate positive thinking as an adult when trying to solve challenging problems.

'I haven't failed: I've just found 10,000 ways that won't work.'
(Thomas Edison. American inventor.)

- The fear of looking silly can stop many people in their track but knowing that everyone makes mistakes will encourage the child to take risks. Mistakes teach necessary lessons for life, focus attention on the specific areas of weakness of a solution, and help the individual to devise better ways of working.

- Encourage children not to take themselves too seriously and to laugh at their mistakes. What is the worst that could happen? Is it so bad? Will it matter in a week, month, or year?

- Explain how athletes use visualisation techniques to help themselves to be brave. Visualisation being the process of creating a mental image of what you would like to happen, to imagine how good you will feel and how happy you will be to achieve your goal.

- Encourage the child to keep away from people who belittle their efforts, and to discuss their aspirations with people who will be encouraging and supportive.

b. Personal bravery. My pteromerhanophobia is getting worse.

Pteromerhanophobia, glossophobia, and acrophobia are the Greek words for: a fear of flying, a fear of public speaking, and a fear of heights. Such phobias are common. A quarter of the population suffer from a fear of flying, three quarters from a fear of public speaking, and a sixth from a fear of heights.

Individuals can have numerous other less common phobias. I once went with a friend to a conference at York University. It took us over an hour to walk from the university car park to the conference centre, a distance of 200 metres, because of my friend's duck phobia. The campus was full of water features and a variety of different water fowl mingled with the students; waddling across paths, pooping in the green spaces, and quacking in the bushes. My friend refused to go anywhere near them, and our progress towards the conference centre was slow, haphazard, and involved the requisition of a laundry cart.

I'm frightened of flying, which in a way is easier, because planes are in the sky and can be avoided. I think this particular fear has roots in Saturday morning children's cinema. In between throwing objects at the mob in the stalls, and cheering on the Lone Ranger and Tonto, the entertainment would always include an exciting extract from war film. As a result, deep in my subconscious is the certainty that when you venture into the skies above the Channel, the Luftwaffe will be waiting to strafe your plane just as soon as the sun is in the pilot's eyes.

A few years ago, I decided it was time to face up to this particular fear and enrolled on Heathrow Airport's 'Fear of Flying' course. I was seduced by their advert, which featured two fit-looking men in uniform, chatting solicitously to an apprehensive, middle-aged, female passenger.

There were several good-looking men in uniform running the course, but all of their solicitous attention was focussed on the one young blonde they had seated with them at the front of the plane, while forty mature women were clumped in a forlorn group at the back. When the plane took off, rather than clinging to the manly forearm of a George Clooney lookalike, I found myself gripping the hands of Maureen and Valerie. Maureen was screaming hysterically and Valerie sobbing uncontrollably.

As I'm such a coward myself, I'm always amazed at the bravery of others, particularly the everyday type of person, who find themselves caught up in terrifying situations. I know if I were ever conscripted into the armed forces, I would constantly question the decisions of my superiors.

'Just a thought, and I'm sure that you know what you're doing, Admiral, but don't you think it would be safer if we kept the shore in sight at all times?'

'I've seen a film of this, Sergeant Major, and I think we need to remember that jungles can be dangerous places.'

When Armistice Day comes around and previous generations talk about their personal experiences of war, I'm always staggered by their bravery. It certainly puts a fear of ducks into perspective.

6. CURIOSITY

a. Developing children's curiosity

'I have no special talent. I am only passionately curious.' (Albert Einstein.)

Children vary in their levels of curiosity. Some children like to find out about things they know nothing about, others are happier to research information that adds to their existing knowledge. A child may ask a thousand questions about the history of the Royal Family and the classification of butterflies but care very little about geographical facts or classical music.

Young children are naturally curious, but some will have been encouraged to ask questions in their early years, while others will have been discouraged.

The education system can repress children's curiosity by favouring right answers over unusual or new answers. If curiosity is not encouraged, there is a danger that children will become passive learners, accepting whatever they are told without question. The more curious a child is, the more creative they will become.

To encourage children's curiosity:

- Encourage children to try something new. Something they would not normally think of doing or have knowledge of. The more understanding of a diverse range of topics the children have, the more unusual and creative links they will be able to make. Do not worry if an obsession with beetles only lasts for a fortnight before morphing into a fascination with Greek myths; the child will acquire a substantial amount of knowledge during that fortnight.

- Young children learn best from observing adults, so model curiosity. Let the child see you research information when you are unsure of an answer. Investigate a topic together, perhaps on the internet, ask another person, or look information up in a magazine or book.

- Reading always sparks curiosity. Discuss the books they are reading. Research information about the illustrator. Read the blurb about the author and see what other books they have written.

- Discuss situations and events broadcast on the television or radio, and interesting articles that you have read in the paper or a magazine.

- Curiosity requires an independence of mind. Give children the freedom to explore those things that interest them.

- Take the children out and about. Visit new places and different environments. This need not mean expensive trips and excursions but could involve walking around the local neighbourhood. Point out things of interest: old buildings, different types of cars, birds, unusual dogs or plants in people's gardens. Walk slowly and take time to observe things in the environment.

- Do routine activities in different ways. Take a different route to or from school, go into different shops in town, have something different for breakfast, go to different parks and green spaces, or take a different route to see relatives.

CHAPTER 3

NEURO-DIVERSITY IN SCHOOLS

INTRODUCTION

'Why fit in when you were born to stand out.' (Dr Seuss.)

Neurodiversity is a term used to describe the variety of ways in which individual brains function, and different children think, learn, and behave. Those who perform within the parameters of what society judges to be 'normal' are referred to as being neurotypical. Individuals who fall outside these norms are referred to as being neurodivergent.

Many children are only judged to be neurodivergent when in school; within family and social environments they would be seen to be neurotypical.

The benefits of expanding the understanding of 'normal' neurological behaviour, particularly within education systems, would include:

✓ Children are all individual, with different personalities, approaches to learning, levels of motivation, and underlying abilities. It would be preferable to focus on the children's talents and strengths, rather than on their perceived deficiencies.

✓ An acknowledgement of neurodiversity would align with society's increasing acceptance of racial, religious, and cultural diversity.

Everyone is responsible for the barriers faced by others in society, and many of the challenges neurodivergent children face arise from systems that focus on a narrow definition of 'normal' behaviour.

✓ The numbers of children described as being neurodivergent have increased dramatically over recent years. It would be unreasonable to portray such a large group in negative ways.

1. INCLUSION IN SCHOOLS

a. Individual differences in the classroom: home/school liaison

All teachers are trained to recognise, and expected to provide for, the differing and individual needs of every child in their care. This expectation should be met by what is referred to as 'Quality First Teaching'. QFT could be defined as teaching that delivers high-quality teaching to every single child in a school.

When a teacher first registers concerns about a child's performance or behaviour, they will try to identify the root of the problem in order to best help the child. Parents are in a unique position to provide additional information to the school about their child. The teacher will see the child as one pupil within a large group and will not have the benefit of the family's in-depth knowledge of their son or daughter.

It is essential to establish the root cause of any difficulty if the support the teacher gives a child is going to be effective. When the parent is alerted by teachers to the fact that their child has a problem with, for example, attention and focus in the classroom, this could be explained in several ways. The child may:

• Have a temporary hearing loss. It may appear to teaching staff that the child is not bothering to pay attention, but if the parents inform the school that their child suffers from regular colds, which lead to glue ear and intermittent deafness, teaching staff will be able to make allowances.

- Have less of a concentration span than the adult expects. Children's concentration span is approximately two-three minutes per year of their age. Therefore, an average six-year-old would be able to concentrate for between 12-18 minutes, and an average 10-year-old for between 20-30 minutes. If the child's concentration span is below average, and the teacher's expectation of the classes' attention span is unrealistic, many of the pupils will be judged to have a problem with focus and attention.

- Have a poor memory. When the child with a weak memory cannot answer a question in class, it may appear to the teacher that they have not been listening. However, the family may have noticed that the child becomes confused when given a lot of information at the same time.

'Please could you go upstairs to the back bedroom and bring down my green shoes. I think they're in the bottom of Dad's wardrobe.'

The child will remember part of the instructions, go upstairs and then be at a loss as to what to do next. Such confusion would suggest an underlying memory weakness and is information that should be shared with the school.

- Have slow processing skills. If a teacher gives information or instructions too quickly for the child to be able to process, they will give up trying to understand what is being said, and it will appear to the teacher that if they have not been listening. However, parents may have learnt that it is better to give the child one instruction before adding the next, or to repeat information several times.

When families and schools share information, outcomes will improve for the children.

b. Quotes from school reports

Huge numbers of children have skills and qualities that go unrecognised in school.

➢ John Lennon. Musician.

'Certainly on the road to failure.'

➢ Stephen Fry. Comedian, playwright, novelist.

'He has glaring faults and they have certainly glared at us this year.'

➢ Siegfried Sassoon. Poet.

'Lacks power of concentration, shows no particular intelligence or aptitude for any branch of his work.'

➢ Eric Morecambe. Comedian.

'This boy will never get anywhere in life.'

➢ Sue Lawley. Radio presenter.

'Susan would do well not to distract her friends during class.'

➢ Dame Judi Dench. Actress.

'Judi would be a good pupil if she lived in this world.'

➢ Nick Park. Creator of 'Wallace and Gromit'.

'Inclined to dream. Could do better if he tried.'

➢ Sir Norman Wisdom. Actor.

'The boy is every inch a fool, but luckily for him he is not very tall.'

➢ Beryl Bainbridge. Novelist and playwright.

Geography. 'Her knowledge of the subject is so poor as to make one wonder if she is simple-minded.'

➢ Winston Churchill. Politician.

'He is so regular in his irregularity, that I really don't know what to do.'

c. Quotes: my school experiences

Large groups of children do not feel comfortable within the school system.

o Winston Churchill. Politician.

'How I hated school, and what a life of anxiety I lived there.'

o Margaret Mead. Anthropologist.

'My grandmother wanted me to have an education, so she kept me out of school.'

o Thomas Edison. Inventor.

'I was at the foot of my class.'

o Beatrix Potter. Author.

'Thank goodness I was never sent to school; it would have rubbed off some of the originality.'

o Woody Allen. Actor.

'I loathed every day and regret every moment I spent in school.'

o Dolly Parton. Singer and song writer.

'I hated school.'

o Bertrand Russell. Philosopher.

'Men are born ignorant, not stupid; they are made stupid by education.'

o H.H. Munro. Writer.

'You can't expect a boy to be vicious till he's been to a good school.'

o Robert Frost. Poet.

'Education is hanging around until you've caught on.'

o Mark Twain. Writer.

'I have never let my schooling interfere with my education.'

d. Medical and social models of disability

In the medical model of disability, disability is viewed in medical terms, and any difficulties the individual experiences are considered to be something to be treated through medical intervention.

The social model of disability considers individuals to be disabled by society. For example, society could minimise the disadvantage experienced by the visually impaired by making accommodation and adaptations in schools, shops, offices, public transport, and city and cultural centres.

It is interesting to note that different countries report varying levels of neurodiversity within their population. In 2019 Hong Kong identified 372 ASC children in every thousand youngsters, South Korea 263, Denmark 69, Germany 38, the UK 11, and Poland 3. Such differences cannot be due to a greater understanding of ASC or more comprehensive diagnostic systems but must reflect alternative cultural expectations of children's behaviour.

Problems are not always within the child but may lie within the environment in which the child finds themselves. The challenges children face in school will be reduced by a greater understanding of their intellectual and emotional profile, appreciation of their strengths and talents, and a greater flexibility of the education system.

e. School support. Quality First Teaching

All teachers in the UK are expected to provide Quality First Teaching, that is high-quality, inclusive teaching for every child in their care. Children will require differentiation to meet their individual learning needs. Differentiation could be defined as, 'the use of a range of teaching approaches designed to meet the needs of different learners in the same class'.

Examples of effective differentiation strategies

The problem – Copying quickly and accurately from the board

When copying from the whiteboard, X finds it confusing if the teacher talks about new information at the same time.

While some children will learn information by writing facts out, all of X's energy will be focused on the practical effort of copying, rather than on remembering and learning the information.

Many children have poor working memories, making copying accurately from the board difficult and time-consuming.

It would be preferable for X to be given clear, well-spaced handouts to annotate.

The problem – Confusion and misunderstanding over work and tasks to be completed

X is uncertain of what to do, or how to do it.

Make all instructions concise and clear, so X knows exactly what is required.

Encourage X to seek clarification when unsure and respond positively to X's questions.

Use 'scaffolding' to demonstrate appropriate approaches, and the type of response that is expected to work set. (Scaffolding being the process whereby teachers demonstrate exactly how to solve a problem or set out work, giving examples for reference. The adult gradually withdraws the scaffold as the pupil's understanding of the desired format increases.)

The problem – Self-esteem

X suffers from low self-confidence because of underperformance in the classroom.

Be patient. X may be making the same amount of effort as peers, but with a different outcome each time. Let X know that you understand that they are working hard. Extra effort is a fact of life for some children, but it is gratifying for this to be acknowledged by adults.

Play to X's strengths so that s(he) is able to experience success in the classroom.

X should be encouraged to identify those strategies that s(he) finds helpful. When in doubt, ask X what is most useful by way of support.

The problem – Slow processing speed

X finds it hard to keep up with the speed of lesson delivery and is easily confused by information given orally.

Try to avoid long periods of teacher talk.

Support oral input with visual aids, group work, discussion, and practical activity.

Record information and instructions on the board for pupils to refer back to.

Provide ample opportunities for over-learning and repetition.

X should be allowed extra time to process information before answering questions. X may know the answer but will need time to think of how to structure a response.

If X has slow processing and reads or writes slowly, consider applying for extra time in public exams. Additional time will allow X to read a question carefully, understand what is being asked, plan a response, and write a legible answer.

The problem – A need for targeted marking and formative feedback

X's work is littered with grammatical and spelling errors.

X does not appear to understand how to improve his/her work.

Do not highlight every grammatical or spelling error in X's work. Draw attention to basic and/or regular mistakes.

Provide constructive feedback with precise explanations of <u>how</u> to improve work. Helpful feedback might be, 'Good work. To get a higher mark, make sure you give one quote for every point you make. For example, when you discuss Romeo's naivety, you could quote …' Unhelpful feedback would be, '12/20. Better.' Keep drawing X's attention to your comments.

The problem – Conflict of learning and teaching style

The child finds maintaining their focus in chalk-and-talk lessons difficult.

Use a variety of teaching approaches in order to satisfy different learning preferences: games, group work, discussion, independent research, videos and film clips, photos and diagrams, field trips, practical sessions, role-play, talks, and IT.

The problem – Poor organisation and presentation of work.

Use IT to help X with the organisation and presentation of their work

f. School support. The role of a school's Special Educational Needs and Disability Coordinator (SENDCo).

The Special Educational Needs and Disability Co-ordinator

(SENDCo) of a school has a critical role to play to ensure that every pupil is successfully included in all school and classroom activities.

Every school must have a SENDCo. They must be a qualified teacher, and any newly appointed SENDCo must undertake a National Award in Special Educational Needs Co-ordination within three years of taking up the post.

The responsibilities of a school's SENDCo include:

- Overseeing the day-to-day operation of the school's Special Educational Needs and Disability Policy.

- The identification and monitoring of children who teachers feel may have additional needs.

- Co-ordinating any additional provision required by pupils.

- Liaising with parents.

- Liaising with external agencies: speech and language therapists, occupational therapists, educational psychologists, and other specialists.

- Ensuring that the school has adequate tracking and monitoring system in place.

2. SPECIFIC LEARNING DIFFERENCE/DIFFICULTY (SPLD)

a. What are Specific Learning Differences/Difficulties (SpLDs)?

➤ SpLD is an umbrella term used to cover a range of conditions.

SpLDs include dyslexia, dyspraxia, dyscalculia, Attention Deficit

Hyperactivity Disorder (ADHD), together with some aspects of Autistic Spectrum Condition (ASC).

Specific Learning Differences differ from General Learning Difficulties in that a child with a SpLD will have what is known as a 'spiky profile', that is they will be good at certain things, but average or weak at others. Children with a general learning difficulty will perform at a low level across the board.

As there is no clear cut-off point for a diagnosis, specific learning difficulties are said to exist across a spectrum; a child may experience a mild, moderate, or severe difficulty. Many children experience some degree of dyslexia, dyspraxia, ASC, ADHD, or dyscalculia, but will not meet the criteria for a diagnosis.

Dyslexia associations estimate that between 10% and 16% of the population are dyslexic, with 4% of this group experiencing severe symptoms. This would mean in an average class of 30 children, between three and five children will have some degree of dyslexia.

Points to note:

➤ There is an overlap of symptoms within different SpLDs.

Poor concentration, for example, is a symptom of the several SpLDs, but the root cause in each case may be different.

❖ A child may have poor concentration because of a general weakness of attention. They may be easily distracted by their thoughts, or things that are happening in the classroom; the teacher's shoes squeaking, the pupil asleep in the back row, or a fly buzzing at a window. (ADHD)

❖ A child with sensory processing problems may not be concentrating because they feel too hot or too cold, the classroom may be too noisy, or the science lab too smelly. They will be unable to focus on anything because of their physical discomfort. (Sensory processing weaknesses.)

❖ The vocabulary the teacher is using may be too complex for a child with a language processing weakness. The child has lost the drift of the lesson because they don't understand what is being said, or because the teacher is talking too quickly. (Language difficulty)

❖ The child may have a physical problem such as an undiagnosed hearing loss and, because they only hear snippets of what is going on, they find it hard to focus. (Hearing impairment)

➢ <u>The degree to which a pupil is affected by a learning differences will vary.</u>

Each individual is a complex mix of strengths and weaknesses. A child may be extremely dyslexic, but motivated, hardworking, have a specific talent for music, ICT, design, drama, or art, be sociable and popular with their peers, have sympathetic support at home and a resilient personality. Such a child may go through life frustrated by their inability to spell accurately, remember names, or process information quickly, but will be able to use compensatory strategies, and their overall achievement will not be affected.

Children who succeed at school tend to be logical thinkers who learn through auditory channels, have good levels of concentration, are articulate, listen carefully, and obey instructions. Children with SpLD may be the exact opposite of this.

However, although some personality traits are a disadvantage in school, they can be an asset in other contexts. There are two sides to every story.

A child could be described as:

- Constantly out of seat/energetic and lively.

- Inflexible and pedantic/possesses the ability to focus on detail.

- Deviating from what others are doing/an independent thinker.

- Bossy/holds and defends passionate opinions.

- Disorganised/a creative thinker, who is absorbed in their own ideas.

Many children develop alternative skills as a result of experiencing challenges at school: they will be more tolerant of others and demonstrate empathy and patience towards their peers. They will be fun to be around and able to laugh at themselves.

Exposure to adversity in the school environment could be seen as a good preparation for life. Failure, anxiety, boredom, and embarrassment are everyday occurrences in school for some children. These children will know that it is impossible to die of shame when you get 0/20 in a test, or from disappointment when you fail to get the result you wanted, in spite of making a supreme effort. Pity the poor child who never experiences such situations until they start university or go to work. Unless children meet and cope with frustration and failure in small doses early in life, they will have little confidence in their ability to deal with such emotions as they grow up.

b. Sensory issues. Vision.

When a child is experiencing any unexpected difficulty at school, physical and sensory issues should be the first area to be investigated.

Visual difficulties can affect a child's performance in the classroom but may go undetected in routine eye examinations or school-based screenings. Some children will need an assessment from an optometrist.

An optometrist is a doctor who examines eyes and diagnoses eye problems.

An optician measures an individual's vision, and fits glasses and contact lenses.

All children under the age of 16, and teenagers under the age of 19 in full-time education, are entitled to free NHS sight tests, as well as help with the cost of glasses or contact lenses.

One example of a common visual problem would be convergence insufficiency.

Convergence insufficiency occurs when a child's eyes do not work together effectively when focusing on close objects. This misalignment involves the muscles that move the eye. The condition causes blurred or double vision.

Signs of convergence insufficiency include:

- Tired or uncomfortable eyes, leading to a reluctance to read or do other close work.

- Headaches that lead to a reluctance to read or do other close work.

- Difficulties with reading. Words may seem to move about the page, the child may lose their place or read very slowly. A child may read complex, long words easily, but omit or reverse smaller words: 'no' becoming 'on', 'was' becoming 'saw'.

- Blurred or double vision. The child may not mention experiencing a problem, as they assume that they are seeing what everyone else sees.

- The child's work may be untidy and messy.

- The child may appear clumsy and physically awkward.

   Treatment. Simple eye-focusing exercises, as prescribed by an optometrist.

c. Sensory issues. Irlen Syndrome/Scotopic Sensitivity Syndrome.

Irlen Syndrome, or Scotopic Sensitivity Syndrome, is a visual perceptual difficulty that affects the way the individual's brain processes visual information. The Irlen Syndrome Foundation estimates that 14% of children experience scotopic sensitivity, with nearly half of all children with a specific learning difference being affected.

Children suspected of experiencing scotopic sensitivity may exhibit some of the following symptoms:

- Visual discomfort, headaches, and difficulties with concentration when working under bright or fluorescent light. The child may prefer to read in a dim light.

- The child finds natural sunlight dazzling and uncomfortable. They will be bothered by glare even on a hazy day.

- The child may complain of headaches and dizziness when reading for a prolonged period of time.

- Difficulties with reading when texts are printed on glossy white paper, or notes written on a shiny whiteboard.

- A general difficulty in reading print, numbers, or musical notation. Words, numbers, or musical notes appear to shift, merge, wobble, fade, or move about on the page.

- The child may look away from a book, shake their head or rub their eyes before looking back.

- The white background of a page appears to dominate, and the black print of the text to fade. The child may express a preference for older books with creamy-coloured paper and reduced paper/print contrast.

- The child may be generally clumsy, with an apparent inability to judge 3D dimensions or distance accurately.

Support strategies:

- As Scotopic Sensitivity Syndrome is a visual processing problem rather than an optical weakness, the child will need to be assessed by an optometrist rather than an optician.

- Some children will find coloured overlays, or glasses with coloured lenses, helpful for reading. Coloured overlays placed over text may help the child by reducing the contrast between black print and the white page. Overlays can be made from coloured plastic A4 sheets that can be bought at most High Street stationers.

- Coloured file paper can help with written work. The most suitable colour will depend on individual preference, but a pale green or pale blue seem to be popular shades.

- School staff can help by changing background colours on computer screens, or printing handouts on pastel-coloured paper. Most children seem to prefer an off-white, creamy colour, or a pale shade of blue or green.

- Wearing sunglasses or a peaked cap will help with glare both indoors and outdoors.

d. Sensory issues. Hearing difficulties

It is important to rule out any hearing difficulty as a reason for poor academic performance. A hearing loss will affect the child at home and school and will need following up with the family's GP.

Some children will have an intermittent hearing loss, the most common of these being glue ear. Glue ear occurs when the individual has frequent colds or a runny nose. The middle ear fills with fluid and hearing is impaired.

If episodes of glue ear coincide with a time when the child is acquiring sound to symbol correspondence, the ability to differentiate between similar sounds may be affected. The letters 'p', 'd' and 'b' will all sound the same to a child with a heavy cold. Children may not be aware of their difficulty and, as the hearing loss is intermittent, the problem may not be picked up by the usual hearing checks.

Typical behaviour from a child with a hearing weakness would include: leaning forward to catch what is being said; watching a speaker's lips closely; asking for information to be repeated; an apparent lack of attention; regular ear-ache; tiredness; indistinct speech; poor pronunciation; a monotonous speech pattern. The child may seem confused as if they are unaware of what is going on and be constantly watching other children for clues and then following their lead.

'Everyone is standing up. Where are we going? Why are they collecting their coats? What are they getting out of their lockers? Are we going outside?'

The child with a hearing problem may have a difficulty acquiring and developing vocabulary. If they do not hear unfamiliar words correctly, they will have little idea of how to pronounce the words, or what the words will look like in print.

The listening comprehension of a child with hearing problems is likely to be underdeveloped because of the unreliability of information input; sometimes they will hear and sometimes not. They are certain to have patchy knowledge and understanding as a result.

3. DYSLEXIA

a. Dyslexia in the Primary School

Dyslexia is often described as a learning difference rather than learning difficulty to emphasise the fact that the condition is common to the point of being banal. Celebrities regularly discuss their dyslexia in the media: Steve Jobs, Keira Knightley, Tom Cruise, Orlando Bloom, Jennifer Aniston, Paloma Faith, Steven Spielberg: the list goes on.

It is estimated that between 10% and 16% of the UK population have some degree of dyslexia, therefore in every class of thirty pupils, at least three children will have dyslexic tendencies.

Dyslexia exists on a continuum from mild to severe. The different learning styles of the majority of dyslexic children can be easily accommodated in the classroom, with any differentiation that helps the dyslexic child, benefitting every other child in the class.

Indicators of dyslexia in a KS1/KS2 child include:

- Slow acquisition of literacy skills

  The child will be slow to develop reading and writing skills, although they appear bright and articulate.

- Slow processing

  The children need extra time to process and make sense of information. They may need to go over facts several times before they gain a secure understanding. These children will get there, but in their own time.

- A weak memory

  The child may forget the names of things and people, and use words like 'thingy-mijig', 'whatsit' and 'what's-her-name'.

  They will have a difficulty recalling sequences such as the alphabet, days of the week, or months of the year.

- A poor appreciation of rhyme

  The child has a difficulty recognising rhyming sounds and words.

- Sequencing problems

  When pronouncing words, children with dyslexia may change the order of sounds within the word, for example, 'par cark' for 'car park'.

Many young dyslexics will experience an overlap with other conditions:

- Co-ordination, (dyspraxia). The child's fine motor skills may be slow to develop. They may be late to learn how to hold a pencil, do up buttons, and tie shoelaces. They may not establish a dominant hand in the same way as their peers, happily writing, cutting, throwing, and painting with left or right hand.

- Number, (dyscalculia). Learning number bonds, times tables, and telling the time may give the dyslexic child additional difficulty.

It is easy to see how apparently isolated and small irritations can combine to create wider problems for the child. The fact that slow processing of instructions, a poor memory, and weak sequencing skills will lead to organisational problems should not be a surprise to anyone.

Parent: 'Remember to bring home your spellings tonight to learn for the test on Thursday.'

Child: 'Remember to bring home … remember to bring what home?' (Slow processing.) 'Don't know. I can't remember what she said.' (Poor memory.) 'What day is the spelling test? What day is it tomorrow?' (Weak sequencing skills.)

It is important to bear in mind that dyslexic children are classic late developers. This can be useful when offering the children reassurance. Life is a marathon, not a sprint.

b. Dyslexia in the secondary school

The following behaviours would be observed in an older child with dyslexic tendencies. _(Possible solutions are in italics.)_

➢ Hesitant reading, adding words, repeating words, skipping lines, re-reading lines, or losing their place in a text altogether.

Use a small ruler to put under the line they are reading. Move the ruler down to the next line after they have read the first. Tracking the sentence in this way with a pen may seem preferable to an older child when reading in front of others.

➢ Having to read a passage several times to access the meaning. Read once to decode the words, read again for fluency, and read again in order to understand the text.

Use the Text to Speech facility on a computer to hear material read aloud.

Use Listening Books or CDs to read set texts.

Apply for an extra time allowance in public exams to give the child additional time to read exam papers. Or, if the child's reading difficulty is more severe, apply for a reader for a child. (A reader being an adult who reads the exam paper and the questions to a child.)

➢ Spelling a word in several different ways in the same piece of writing.

Word process as much work as possible and use the spell checker.

Concentrate on spelling important subject-specific words correctly. An English teacher may forgive 'consederation' but will not forgive 'Shakspeer'.

Keep a notebook handy listing the correct spelling of any words the child has a consistent problem with and encourage them to use the book for reference.

➢ Difficulty in remembering basic grammar and punctuation. The child's work will be littered with commas, hyphens, and semi colons, depending on what the focus was in the English lesson that week, or recent corrections made to their work.

Try to persuade them that simple is best. The aim of written work is to communicate with others. Keep it straight forward. Use short sentences.

➢ Rambling and going off the point in written work.

Provide a 'scaffold' for an appropriate essay structure in that particular subject and explain the scaffold. The format that an English essay should take may be obvious to an English teacher, but not to a Year 7 pupil. A scaffold is a prompt that the child can use to structure their History/English Literature/R.E. essay in the desired format. For example, PEE for a basic essay: make your Point, provide the Evidence and give an Explanation.

➢ Experiencing good days and bad days for no apparent reason. This may be due to tiredness because of the extra effort required from the child to keep pace with their peers, or the child may be using different skillsets on different days. They may have excellent skills in one area and zero degree of ability in another: their performance will depend on which skillset they are using at that moment in time. No-one will know which skills are being used, least of all the child.

The adult must be understanding and patient. Criticism will not necessarily bring improvement.

➢ Poor self-esteem. Despite trying hard, the child will be functioning below their potential.

Recognition by the adult of the child's level of effort.

Adults should focus on areas in which the child can succeed in order to play to their strengths and boost their confidence. This can be within or outside school: perhaps recognising the child's talents within the classroom; any personal and social talents that can be used within school; or associations and clubs they participate in: choirs, computer, gardening, drama, art, cookery or sport clubs, church groups or organised voluntary work.

➢ Poor handwriting. Handwriting is often small and indistinct to try to hide weak spelling.

The child should be encouraged to word process their work and learn to touch type. When this is recognised as the child's normal way of working, they will be allowed to word process in public exams.

➢ Poor organisation. As a result of a poor memory, the child will forget sports kit, textbooks, return slips, homework, and appointments with members of staff.

Use Apps on phones to provide reminders.

Organise school bags the previous evening against a checklist.

Keep spare sets of equipment in several places.

Make a list of tasks to be done, perhaps written on a whiteboard in their bedroom, and encourage the child to review and update the list daily.

Keep timetables in several places at home and school.

Label everything.

➤ A difficulty with expressing themselves succinctly. They can't quite recall the name of something, somewhere, or someone. The child may start a sentence hoping that the necessary words will come to them as they speak, but if they don't, they will be left struggling with a half-formed contribution to discussions. The child then has a choice; should they try to express an opinion or never ever speak. Other children's ideas seem to follow a logical sequence like a ball of string. The dyslexic child's ideas will be just as valuable but collected in their head like a pile of spaghetti.

Patience and sympathetic encouragement on behalf of the listener.

Alternative approaches to class discussions could be tried; perhaps the children could formulate their ideas and plan their response within pairs or small groups, before delivering them to the whole class.

➤ Excessive tiredness due to the amount of additional effort required from the child to keep up with their peers. A dyslexic pupil will find it hard to work automatically; every aspect of a task will demand their attention. When taking notes, they will have to listen, sort out the important facts that need to be recorded, remember these facts and note them down neatly enough to read later, spell correctly, all whilst listening and sifting subsequent pieces of information. Most children do this automatically: the dyslexic child will have to concentrate on every activity.

Teaching staff should make efforts to accommodate the child's needs. In the case of note taking, for example, a sheet of lesson notes could be provided for the child to annotate and highlight; the teacher could allow the child to make a recording of the lesson; or another student's work could be photocopied.

Ensure the child gets an adequate amount of sleep.

c. Memory

There are several types of memory, including:

- <u>Short-term memory.</u> Short-term memory works with information that has to be retained for a limited period of time: a phone number, a car registration number, or an address.

- <u>Long-term memory.</u> Long-term memory is like a filing cabinet. Information to be stored will be divided into facts and personal experiences: the dates of friends' birthdays, last year's holiday, or information about a favourite band.

- <u>Working memory.</u> Working memory manipulates one piece of information while holding other pieces of information in mind, moving attention backwards and forwards between the two. For example, when tackling a Maths problem, the child will need to recall number bonds and times tables, while working through the sequence necessary to solve the problem.

Why children forget

- Anxiety. When children are anxious, their learning will be superficial.

- The child may not be concentrating. Attention is essential if information is to be retained.

- Information will be forgotten unless it is reviewed and revisited regularly to establish it securely in long-term memory. This 'memory fade' is known as the Ebbinghaus Forgetting Curve. Ebbinghaus, a German psychologist, discovered that 80% of the information an individual learns is lost within 24 hours if it is not reviewed.

- When children try to rote learn information that they haven't understood, the facts may merge into a confusing mass.

- A lack of interest. Children may have little interest in the topic or see the subject as being irrelevant.

- Physical discomfort: tiredness, hunger, thirst, being too hot or too cold.

- The child may not like the subject, the set of children they are with, or the teacher.

d. Working memory

Working memory capacity varies from child to child. Research shows that in any class of eight-year-old children, 10% of the children have the working memory of an average five-year-old, and 10% have that of an adult. The other pupils will have a working memory capacity that is somewhere between these two extremes.

A link between a good working memory and academic achievement has always been recognised. A limited working memory can be a significant disadvantage in school, particularly when the implications are not appreciated by teaching staff.

Children with a poor working memory will need to be aware of this weakness, and put strategies into place to help themselves:

o To carry a notebook in their bag or pocket and use the book to jot information down: Remember to bring kit for cricket match tomorrow. Remember to bring flute for extra rehearsal on Friday. Get Mum to fill in Parents' Evening slip tonight.

o To use apps on their phones as reminders.

o To make good use of diaries, calendars, and lists.

o To work using paper, rather than trying to manipulate detail and facts mentally. This will free up the child's memory to retain the overview.

Teachers can help in lessons by giving short, concise instructions; noting information on the board for children to refer back to; and by using collaborative working so that children with good memories can repeat instructions for their peers. All strategies that reduce overload on the children's working memory will be beneficial.

e. Slow processing

A poor working memory and slow processing speed can combine to create a double whammy for some children.

Processing speed refers to the rate at which the individual is able to take information in, make sense of it, and respond appropriately. Children with slow processing will always be slightly out of step with others. By the time they have worked out what someone meant by what they said, the conversation will have moved on and they will have been left behind.

The situation will be more challenging for the children if they have to quickly process several things at the same time; for example, a long list of instructions:

Teacher: 'Please can you open your green textbooks and turn to page 193. Read the introduction to Section C and do all of the odd numbered questions. After question 9, turn to the back of the book and check your answers, then, if you have all of the questions correct, you can go on to page 204, and start working your way through the problems.'

Teachers can help children in school by:

❖ Checking the child's understanding discreetly. Have an agreement that the child can signal for help if they are confused.

❖ Allowing extra time to answer questions. Warn the child that they will be asked a question soon to give them time to prepare their answer.

'I want you all to think of two solutions. Holly, I'll ask you for your ideas after we've passed the photos round.'

❖ Trying to reduce the need for multi-tasking by, for example, writing instructions in bullet points on the board for the children to refer to as they work.

❖ Using paired and group working. Instructions will then be repeated several times and clarified by peers.

❖ Encouraging children to ask questions when they are uncertain and responding positively to such questions.

❖ Using starters and plenaries to recap on previous sessions, set the scene for the current lesson, and summarise work covered so far.

❖ Using differentiated tasks to revisit and reinforce information in different ways.

❖ Giving clear, unambiguous directions for how all work is to be approached.

4. NUMERACY

a. Helping children with Numeracy

Maths can be a difficult subject for many children. The Maths curriculum is packed with different topics, and if the child does not have enough time to cover a topic satisfactorily, or to practise the necessary methods, they can become confused and anxious.

Common difficulties with Maths include:

1. A poor automatic recall of basic number bonds and times tables.

Solutions.

o Use computer sites or apps to play games that provide lots of non-threatening practice.

o Use musical tapes or times table stories for over learning.

o Use number squares and practical apparatus for concrete and visual support.

o To help the children with estimation, encourage them to learn the easier times table. If they know their 2, 5, 10, and 11 times tables, they will be able to work out approximate answers. Then, when using a calculator, they will have a rough idea of the number they are expecting and be less likely to accept a ridiculous answer.

'6 x 12 will be a bit more than 6 x 11, which is 66. Therefore 6 x 12 will be about 70.'

Estimation is important because many children will trust a

calculator over their own common sense, believing that the calculator is always right. Would one litre of milk really cost £3,008.36? If it takes a car 30 minutes to travel 20 kms, would it really take five minutes for the same car to travel 1,200 kms?

o Use a pencil with the times tables printed on the barrel for quick reference.

2. The child finds it difficult to 'translate' problems. The actual sum may be quite simple, but the wordy presentation confuses them.

<u>Solutions</u>

o When puzzles are wordy, diagrams and pictures will help the children's understanding. Encourage the child to sketch a picture of the problem to help them to make sense of what they are being asked to do.

o Ask the child to read the question aloud and break it down into parts. When they understand three of the four parts of a sum, it will seem easier.

o Enlarge compact text to make it clearer.

o Use practical apparatus, for example, a small clock face with turning hands to work out problems involving time. If the child uses the clock face for a while, they will begin to be able to imagine turning the hands of the face without the need for the actual clock, perhaps using a drawing of the clock face to bridge the move from practical apparatus to working the problem out mentally.

o Highlight any unfamiliar words and work out what they mean. Keep examples of some calculations that use these words to refer back to.

o Discuss the how and why of a calculation before carrying it out. Sharing ideas with others will often clarify confusions.

3. A need for over-learning and repetition.

Solutions

o Use board games to practise basics in a non-threatening way.

o Collect puzzles from newspapers and comics. Many children's magazines include a page of number games.

o There are several numeracy programmes that can be used by children on an individual basis. One good example would be 'The Power of Two' (www.powerof2.co.uk). This programme revises basic number bonds in a repetitive, cumulative way. Other resources in the same series include: Plus 1, Perform with Time, Perform with Times Tables.

o Play card games. Most of these games can be accessed electronically, so the child can compete against themselves and go at their own pace.

o Use IT programmes: Number Shark, Times Tables Rock Stars, Mathletics.

4. A lack of concentration resulting in careless errors.

Solutions.

o Talking calculators can provide an auditory prompt for children. It is easy for children to imagine they are typing in 19 x 2 into the calculator, but type in 91 x 2 instead. The fact that the calculator says the numbers as they are entered will alert the child to any careless slips. Talking calculators are available from the RNIB online shop. Apps on the phone or computer will provide the same support.

o Untidy layout of work leading to unnecessary errors. Use graph or squared paper to keep work ordered and legible.

o Teach the child to record systematically rather than try to do calculations quickly in their head. Some children will complain that recording work is boring, but this approach will help to prevent the mistakes that will lose them marks.

5. A lack of confidence.

<u>Solutions.</u>

o Stress to the child that it is acceptable to make errors, and that these should be seen as a part of learning.

o Encourage the child to think outside the, 'there-must-be-a-mathematical-formula-that-I-don't-understand-for-this' box, and to use their common sense.

o Some children will be slower workers because of the level of their other skills: poor short-term memory, slow processing or sequencing problems. In a competitive environment the child may decide that it is preferable not to compete rather than always to be the last to finish. This may lead to a lack of effort or an attempt to complete work as quickly as possible with the correct answer, (perhaps by cheating), but with no understanding.

It is important to stress that speed is not an essential component of mathematical ability. It is possible to be an excellent mathematician without always being the first person with their hand up. In many ways, children who are a little slower are more thoughtful and open to considering and applying the strategies of others.

If a child experiences a severe problem with Maths that would be considered unusual for a child of their age and general ability, they may be referred for a dyscalculia assessment. A child with dyscalculia would have a pronounced and ongoing difficulty with basic mathematical processes, such as: counting backwards, concepts of time, remembering times tables and number bonds, and a poor understanding of place value.

5. DYSPRAXIA

a. What is Dyspraxia?

All children are individual and every child with dyspraxia will have different sets of strengths and weaknesses. However, the dyspraxic child's main problem will relate to the organisation of their physical movement. Dyspraxia used to be known as 'Clumsy Child Syndrome' because of this.

The child may:

- Be over boisterous when being affectionate, or complain that they have been hit rather than touched.

- Be the last among their peers to learn to ride a bicycle, skip with a rope, roller skate and acquire gross motor skills (hopping, jumping, climbing, and skipping).

- Use the whole of their body for a single movement, for example, jumping when throwing a ball.

- Be uncertain of how much effort is required for a task, appearing heavy-footed and generally to crash about.

- Be untidy in appearance: food split down their jumper, smears on their glasses, hair uncombed, and their shoelaces undone. This may cause problems with their peers, particularly during adolescence, when physical appearance is a key to acceptance.

- Misjudge how close other children and adults are, and bump into them. Growth spurts can increase the children's clumsiness during childhood and adolescence.

- Be slow to learn how to dress themselves and always last to change for PE, swimming, and Games.

- Have difficulties with clear speech because of poor control of the small muscles in their mouth. Many dyspraxic children will have had speech therapy when they were younger.

- Have problems with toileting and personal hygiene.

- Personal organisation may be weak. These children will regularly lose stationery, items of uniform, homework, and letters and forms sent between home and school.

- Appear incapable of producing neat work. Most of the children will experience a difficulty with handwriting. The child's fine motor control will be poor, with difficulty in controlling a mouse in ICT, using tools in DT, drawing maps and diagrams accurately, and using equipment and tools in Science and DT.

- Become frustrated when adults correct them for things they are unable to improve: clumsiness, presentation of work, or lack of verbal fluency.

b. How to help the dyspraxic child

- If the child has glasses, make sure they always wear them and that the lenses are clean.

- Label all items of clothing and equipment.

- Buy clothing that is easy to put on. Less buttons and more zips, fewer laces and more Velcro, ties on elastic that can be slipped over the head, and polo shirts rather than shirts with buttons.

- Reassure the child that they will learn how to dress independently, ride a bike, swim, organise their homework, and that they just need extra practice. They will get there, but in their own time. Such is life: everyone finds some skills harder to acquire than others.

- Be proactive regarding personal hygiene as this is a problem that may leave the child open to teasing. Encourage them to bath or shower regularly and teach them how to work methodically down their body to dry themselves.

- As a parent, be extra vigilant of safety issues. These children are the ones who will walk into trees, fall off the kerb, or knock over shop displays.

- Take every reasonable opportunity to raise the child's self-esteem.

- Use IT to improve presentation, organisation, and planning.

- Neat presentation can be a problem and re-doing untidy work will rarely result in any visible improvement. Therefore, reasonable adjustments will need to be made for the child. For example, if it is essential that the child has a clearly annotated diagram for future reference, teachers could photocopy one for the pupil, or use a template with essential information recorded correctly, but with a few sections left blank for the child to fill in.

- Use 'scaffolds' to structure work and to show the child exactly how to organise their work. How to plan an essay, order their argument, or answer an exam question. Provide examples of what would constitute a good essay, a good set of notes, or a good exam answer.

- Research triangular pens and pencils, left-handed equipment, pencil grips and any other aids you think the child might find helpful.

- Show the child how to use lists to organise themselves; ticking off work they have completed and adding tasks still to be tackled.

c. The dyspraxic child and sport

Encourage any sporting activity the child expresses an interest in. They may never become an elite performer, but any activity that involves physical movement will improve their co-ordination and motor skills.

Swimming will help the child to get a feel of the position of different parts of their body.

Cycling and dancing will improve balance and co-ordination. Horse riding will improve posture and balance. When the child enjoys such activities, extra practice will be fun and not a chore.

For the younger child, mini-circuits in the garden will help to develop balance, co-ordination, timing, and strengthen arm and leg muscles. For example:

➤ Put an evenly spaced line of stones on the garden path for the child to slalom/hop/jump around.

➤ Lay the washing line down on the lawn for the child to walk along with one foot either side. Use the prop for the washing line for the child to balance along without stepping on to the grass too many times.

➤ Any outdoor toys: cones, hoops, large balls, bats, small balls, bean bags can be used to make an exercise course.

Stand two/three/four steps away from a hoop and throw the beanbags into the hoop. How many beanbags can you throw inside the hoop in thirty seconds/one minute?

Kick a ball between two cones ten times, gradually reducing the distance between the cones. How many goals can you score?

Bat a ball into the air or against a wall three/four/five times in a row.

Outdoor games: swing ball, hopscotch, miniature golf, frisbee, hoopla, or boules will help to develop a child's physical co-ordination in a relaxed and fun way.

Break any more complicated physical activities down into small steps. A determined child will learn how to skip, ride a bike, swim, follow a dance routine, if all the stages of the movement can be learnt separately.

Individual sports may be preferable to team sports because:

✓ Individual sports tend to involve rhythmic and/or repetitive movement: swimming, long-distance running, martial arts, and cycling all repeat the same movements over and over again. Lots of repetition and over-learning will give the dyspraxic child the necessary practice, without making them appear different to their peers.

✓ Individual sports allow the child to progress at their own pace; beating a personal best rather than an opponent.

✓ The child can practise individual sports by themselves. They do not need other team members to join in. This is perfect for the child who will have to practise longer and harder than their peers. No-one needs to know the amount of effort they are making.

✓ Individual sports can involve the child as a member of a team. If the child is a cross-country runner, they can be a team member, but perform as an individual. No one will be relying on them to kick a perfect cross or give a perfect pass during a game.

d. Improving your child's handwriting and presentation

The quality of a child's handwriting will depend on their level of hand control. A child with poor handwriting may have a general problem with fine motor control. (Fine motor skills are those involved in small movements of the hands, fingers, feet, and toes.)

Children with poor fine motor skills will have a particular difficulty with neatness and precision. Their drawings may seem immature, and craft work untidy. They may have a difficulty when dressing themselves (tying shoelaces, buttoning shirts, and doing up ties).

These children will benefit from additional opportunities to play with sand, water, clay or playdoh. All of these activities will strengthen the child's hand and finger muscles.

Paper and pencil activities such as: dot to dots, mazes, puzzles, tracing, colouring, and cutting, will provide useful extra practice for the control of writing implements.

To help with dressing, practical activities where the child has to manipulate small objects will give additional fine motor practice without the child realising: Lego, threading beads, construction toys, sewing, model making, or playing with small figures.

If a child enters senior school with poor handwriting, a balance must be struck between improving the legibility of their work, whilst developing their word-processing skills. The child will have been practising handwriting on a daily basis for years, so any weakness in this skill will not be due to a lack of effort. All adults are expected to word-process their work, so learning to touch type is not a retrograde step or an indication of a lack of persistence, but a valuable life skill.

<u>To help your child with the presentation of work:</u>

- Make sure their hands and writing implements are clean before they start work. Clear enough space to work and tidy away all unnecessary clutter.

- Tell the child to target one aspect of handwriting for improvement at a time. Perhaps concentrating on making writing larger, more appropriately spaced, or crossing 't's and dotting 'i's.

- Encourage the child to choose one style of writing and to stick to it, preferably a simple style without loops or twirls. Decide on one angle or slope to the writing.

- Give the child a pad of paper or a mouse mat to lean on to provide a smooth working surface. Show the child how to use their non-writing hand to steady their paper.

- It is easy for young children to develop a poor writing technique that becomes a habit and can be almost impossible to break. One of these bad habits is an awkward pencil grip. This might not be so important in KS1, when the child is not expected to produce a volume of written work, complete tasks within time limits, or take notes at speed, but will lead to problems in secondary school. Point out to the child how to hold their pencil in a 'tripod' grip; second finger below the barrel of the pencil or pen, with first finger and thumb above and on either side of the barrel for support.

Pencil grips will ensure the child holds the pen or pencil correctly. These grips can be purchased from stationers or online. Spongy grips are useful if the child has a tight grip. Novelty grips in the shape of animals or vehicles can be popular with younger children. Some pens and pencils have grip-shaped barrels.

- Experiment with different types of pens and pencils until the child finds one that makes their work look as neat as possible. Gel pens can be smooth, clean, and give pleasing results.

- If the child's writing is very untidy, encourage them to write on every other line of the paper to separate ascenders (those letters that go above the line such as b, h, l) from descenders (letters that drop below the line such as g, j, y and p) and make their writing more legible to the reader.

- If the children's hands ache because they press too heavily with their pen, suggest that they use a fine felt tip, as these pens require less pressure to mark the paper.

- If they are left-handed, remind them to sit to the left of right-handed children when sharing a desk or table.

- If they have glasses, make sure they wear them.

6. ATTENTION DEFICIT AND HYPERACTIVITY DISORDER (ADHD)

a. What is Attention Deficit Hyperactivity Disorder?

Attention Deficit Hyperactivity Disorder (ADHD) is a condition which gives the individual a difficulty with attention, hyperactivity, and impulsivity.

There are three sub-types of ADHD: poor attention, hyperactive-impulsivity, and a combination of inattention and hyperactivity. All of these three sub-types are referred to as ADHD.

The hyperactive symptoms are more likely to lead to an early diagnosis because they are easily identified. Problems with attention may not be apparent until the child is in secondary school and increased levels of concentration are expected.

Symptoms of ADHD:

A difficulty staying on task, a lack of attention to detail, weak listening skills, poor organisation, avoidance of tasks that are not immediately engaging, losing possessions, forgetfulness, being easily distracted, acting without consideration of consequence, and an apparent inability to learn from mistakes.

Possible causes include:

- A genetic trait. 25% of the child's close relatives will also have ADHD, compared to 5 % of the general population.
- Premature birth.
- A low birth weight.
- Environmental causes, for example, pollution.
- Smoking, alcohol, or drug abuse by the mother during pregnancy.

A diagnosis of ADHD is made through observation of the child's behaviour. The ADHD behaviour will have been apparent before the age of six years, and observed in at least two settings – usually home and school – over a prolonged period of time. Other medical conditions will have been ruled out.

There is no simple one-off diagnostic test for ADHD. Assessment is made by adults close to the child completing a questionnaire. The questionnaire includes such questions as:

✓ Is the child often forgetful in daily activities?

✓ Does the child <u>often</u> talk excessively?

✓ Does the child <u>often</u> fidget or squirm in their seat?

✓ Does the child <u>often</u> have difficulty in waiting their turn?

As can be seen from the questions above, the questionnaire is subjective, and will rely on the adult's perception of the child's behaviour. The child may always behave in the same way, but the adult's response to the behaviour may be different. Some teachers are more tolerant of different types of behaviour, or a subject may lend itself to a more relaxed approach; for example, calling out and being physically active may be unacceptable in the Science Lab, but encouraged on the sports field.

<u>Adults might like to consider:</u>

➢ At what point do a child's personality traits become a disorder?

➢ Is a difference in maturity a disorder? It tends to be the younger or less mature children in a class who will be considered to have problems with their concentration and focus.

➢ Are the normal characteristics of childhood, such as exuberance and energy, being diagnosed as disorders?

<u>b. Supporting children with ADHD in the home</u>

Fact = Parenting children with ADHD can be exhausting.

<u>Generic suggestions for supporting the ADHD child in the home:</u>

▪ Increase the child's opportunities to be physically active. Sport is an effective way to burn off excess energy. Many individuals with ADHD have turned to sport to cope with their restlessness. Michael Phelps (Olympic swimmer), Louis Smith and Simone Biles

(Olympic gymnasts), Carl Lewis (Olympic sprinter), and Michael Jordan (American basketball player) all have a diagnosis of ADHD.

- Children with ADHD benefit from playing outdoors. Natural light will counteract over stimulation from the blue light of TV, computers, mobile phones, iPads, and so forth.

- When dealing with the child with ADHD, try to keep your sense of humour. Listen to the child and be sympathetic. Stay as calm as possible and try to defuse, rather than inflame, situations.

- Ignore unimportant irritations. Pick your arguments: remember that children who need the most affection and attention will often try to get it in the most aggravating ways.

- Encourage honesty. When they are late, have forgotten to do something, or not listened to instructions, owning up immediately will mean less trouble in the long run.

- Provide structure and stability at home with regular bed and mealtimes. All children thrive on predictability and routine. Adequate sleep is particularly important for these children.

- ADHD symptoms will be exacerbated when the children are hungry or thirsty. Try to keep their diet as healthy as possible and avoid too much processed food or fizzy drinks.

- Encourage the child to take up yoga for relaxation, martial arts for self-control, or meditation to improve their focus.

- It can be hard for the child when they receive a lot of negative feedback about their behaviour. They will need plenty of opportunities to participate in activities that provide them with positive feedback.

- All children's self-esteem will improve when they are able to pursue personal interests and hobbies. Let the children try lots of different activities. An interest may only last for a short period of time, or become a lifetime's obsession, but often a collection of apparently random hobbies can come together in unique ways for these individuals.

- Find practical solutions to anything that the child finds problematic.

Help with organisation: demonstrate the use of diaries, planners, and lists.

Put up a large whiteboard in their bedroom so that they can record homework, dates of tests, sports fixtures, music lessons, and friend's birthdays.

Provide the child with a notebook to keep in their jacket pocket or schoolbag for jotting down things they must remember and review the notebook regularly.

Encourage them to use apps on their phone for prompts and reminders.

c. ADHD. Medication. Losing one's mojo.

Prescriptions for Ritalin and other ADHD medications in the UK have more than doubled in the last decade, from 359,100 in 2004 to 922,200 in 2014. In America, ADHD is the second most frequent long-term diagnosis made in children, narrowly trailing asthma, and generating annual pharmaceutical sales worth £5.7 billion.

Children with severe ADHD may be unable to function without medication; others will take medication selectively on occasions when focus is essential; while some children will not require medication, but adaptations to their environment.

Medication does not cure ADHD and will not alleviate the symptoms of inattention in a child when difficulties are due to factors other than ADHD, perhaps a poor memory, slow processing, a limited vocabulary, or sensory issues.

Most children with ADHD who use medication to ease symptoms of restlessness and distractibility report an improvement in their focus. They find themselves more able to organise their thoughts and pay attention to what they should be doing. They can concentrate for longer periods of time on subjects and tasks that bore them. The downside seems to be that their natural exuberance and enthusiasm is repressed. They report losing their sense of humour and fun. One boy I taught who began to take ADHD medication while in sixth form told me of an occasion when he was on a half-term skiing holiday. Dave (not his real name) and a friend had met two sixth formers from a girls' school staying in the same hostel, and been invited back to the girls' room to 'watch a Jurassic Park DVD'. To his friend's utter horror, Dave began to take notes on the different dinosaurs starring in the film, recording their varying attributes: approximate height and weight, dietary habits, claw size, and danger rating … Awkward.

d. ADHD. Filling in gaps.

Teachers make a lot of erroneous assumptions. One of the most common is to assume that when pupils' faces are looking their way, they are absorbing all the information that the teacher is busily imparting. Unfortunately, the reality is often very different. The pupils may have lost concentration and be quietly absorbed in their own little world; they may not have sufficient prior knowledge to make sense of what the teacher is saying; or they simply have no interest in what the adult is talking about. Such absences can occur regularly and over a long period of time.

I had this 'road to Damascus' insight whilst covering a Year 9 RE lesson at a Roman Catholic girls' secondary school. The children were required to fill in a revision worksheet asking questions about Christian Festivals. I assumed the task was simple enough, so hadn't spent much time introducing the work. My assumption proved incorrect when a girl put up her hand to confess that she could never remember when Jesus was born. Was it Christmas or Easter? Apart from a few raised eyebrows in the front row, the rest of the class didn't react, so I felt fairly certain the comment wasn't a deliberate wind-up. I explained about Christmas as best I could, but the girl still looked confused. I asked if I could assist, and she said, 'Er, Easter … burnt at the stake?'

Of course, adults can make similar blunders and, having drifted off or misunderstood basic information, happily fill in gaps themselves, sometimes in unpredictable ways. Upon joining the same school, I was introduced to a teaching nun called Sister Vagina. I did think her name a little risqué but assumed the word Vagina must be Latin or Greek for something holy, and so always referred to her as Sister Vagina in conversation. It was only months later when the nun was mentioned in a newsletter, that I realised her name was Sister Regina.

e. ADHD. Beware when judging books by their covers.

Attention Deficit Hyperactivity Disorder (ADHD) is a developmental difference of the brain that gives rise to a lack of inhibition, poor concentration, carelessness, restlessness, and an intolerance of routine.

In school, children with ADHD can be mind-bogglingly irritating. They will call out, chat, and talk out of turn. They make unnecessary noise, scrape chairs, bang, hum, and whistle; give cheeky or impertinent responses, and demonstrate an apparent inability to control their physical movement.

However, when viewed in an alternative light, deficits can become attributes and disorders strengths. For example, individuals with ADHD:

1. Can hyper-focus when engaged with tasks that interest them.

2. Have rapid fire minds, their brains constantly buzzing with new ideas.

3. Possess endless reserves of energy; often appearing happiest in situations that others would find stressful. On some occasions the child can even seem lethargic, appearing to need a degree of stress to motivate themselves.

4. Have the ability to think of unusual solutions to problems. Their brains do not filter out unnecessary information in the same way that conventional brains do, and so they are able to see problems from a variety of original perspectives.

5. Move on when they fail, distracted by some new attraction, seizing opportunities that might make others fret.

6. Multi-task with ease.

Point 6 as above could be applied to one of my granddaughters. She constantly fidgets and fiddles in the classroom yet possesses a disturbing ability to absorb the content of a lesson as she does so.

During one particularly stressful Year 5 grammar lesson, her poor teacher was at his wits' end, reprimanding her yet again for her unrelenting lack of focus. If she didn't concentrate, she wouldn't understand and therefore be unable to progress academically: English grammar being the cornerstone of the British Empire, etc, etc. For her own benefit, and to prove that she hadn't been paying attention, and to demonstrate how much this would affect her performance, he would hold a class test on the lesson content then and there. My granddaughter did not flinch but accepted the challenge with what must have been rather galling aplomb. She achieved full marks in the test, while not one of her classmates scored above 50%.

Drama and tears all round.

Granddaughter genuinely could not understand why everyone else had done so badly: the teacher was only testing what he'd been talking about moments before.

Her friends couldn't understand how she had done so well and they had bombed, when the teacher had been telling her off for not listening.

The unfortunate teacher realised that no-one in the class had been paying attention with the exception of little Fidget Bridget.

Lesson worth learning = Fidgeting is a method used by children with ADHD to help them to concentrate.

7. AUTISTIC SPECTRUM CONDITION/DISORDER

a. What is Autistic Spectrum Condition/Disorder?

Autistic Spectrum Condition (ASC) or Autistic Spectrum Disorder (ASD) is a developmental disorder that affects communication and behaviour.

Autism is known as a "spectrum" disorder because of the different degrees to which individuals can be affected.

Traditionally children with ASC were assumed to have three specific areas of difficulty: social communication and interaction, restricted interests, and repetitive behaviours. While individual children may not have a severe problem in all of these areas, most will experience some degree of difficulty.

Social communication and interaction. The child will:

- Have a difficulty with the 'to and fro' of conversation.

- Talk excessively about a favourite topic without noticing that others are not interested, or giving them the chance to respond.

- Have limited eye contact.

- Have facial expressions, movements and gestures that do not match what they are saying.

- Have an unusual tone of voice that sounds sing-song, or flat and emotionless.

- Have a difficulty understanding another person's point of view.

- Be unable to predict other people's behaviour.

Restricted interests. The child will:

- Have an intense interest in very specific topics, for example: a particular television series, cricket statistics, science fiction films, video games, or train and bus timetables.

Repetitive behaviours. The child may:

- Repeat certain behaviours over and over again, perhaps saying particular words or favourite phrases.

- Become overly focused on moving objects or parts of objects, for example, repeatedly spinning the wheels of a toy car.

- Become upset by the slightest change of routine: a different route taken to school, a change in the school timetable, or a tidied bedroom with possessions returned to the 'wrong' place. The child feels secure when everything always remains exactly the same.

Many children at the milder end of the spectrum will be viewed as eccentric, rather than diagnosed with a specific problem.

b. Girls and ASC

The early diagnostic ASC assessments were designed for boys, so historically the ratio of boys to girls diagnosed with ASC was significant. Many specialists viewed ASC as being an example of an extreme male brain; one with a preference for systemising over empathising.

It is now accepted that girls are on the ASC spectrum, but that their difficulties manifest themselves in different ways. Girls are more likely to be diagnosed with depression or anxiety than autism. However, their depression and anxiety will occur as a result of their ASC, rather than exist in isolation.

As a diagnosis of ASC requires symptoms to be seen in different settings (for most children this would be home and school), girls are less likely to meet the criteria for a diagnosis. Many girls manage to control their fear and panic at school, but then let rip when they get home.

Girls on the spectrum will have a tendency towards perfectionism, and if they are educated in a high-achieving environment, this will aggravate their anxiety. This anxiety will manifest itself in different ways; some girls will withdraw, while others will act out.

ASC girls tend to have a few close friendships, rather than a wide circle of friends This can create problems when friendships come to a natural end, or if friends move to other schools or on to university.

c. Managing anxiety

Unusual levels of anxiety are often seen in children with ASC. The children can become overly anxious in situations that would not bother other children of the same age.

- Separation anxiety. This is a specific worry about separating from family members and can make going to school a traumatic experience.
- Social anxiety. This anxiety involves mixing with other people outside the immediate family. Will anyone like me? What will I say to them? Will they want to make friends? What if they tease or bully me?
- Specific phobias. These phobias can cover a multitude of different things: dogs, thunderstorms, fireworks, birds, snakes, spiders, or noisy hand dryers.

The children's reaction to their anxiety can be extreme: lashing out, undressing, screaming, or running away. Such reactions are commonly referred to as meltdowns. Meltdowns will develop very quickly, and the child will move from calm to alarm within seconds. If their panic is viewed as distress rather than naughtiness, stubbornness, or challenging behaviour, it becomes easier to understand and manage.

- When a child tries to avoid an activity because they are apprehensive, try to appreciate they are not being difficult, awkward, or attention-seeking.
- Stay calm if you can see the child is beginning to get worried: they will get more agitated if you get upset or angry.
- When the child starts to become emotional, try to distract them by directing their attention elsewhere, or find a safe and quiet place where they can calm down.
- Try to work out what the triggers for the behaviour are: what sparks the extreme reaction.
- Help them to face their fears gradually through small-step exposure.
- Praise any efforts the child makes to be brave.
- When the child has regained self-control, try to work out with the child exactly why they were frightened, and what it is that they are worried about. Talk about the perceived threat. Is it a real threat? How could they try to deal with it?
- Help them to think of ways to self-calm, for example, using headphones to listen to a favourite CD.

d. Anger management

Many children are slow to develop self-control and need additional help in developing anger-management techniques.

Work with your child to devise a plan of action to avoid getting into trouble at home and school.

- Discuss what things trigger their anger. If the child knows that they are short-tempered when they are hungry, anxious, or in noisy or hot environments, they may be able to deal with the situation, remove themselves, or put avoidance strategies into place before losing their temper.

- There may be outward signs that the child is beginning to lose self-control. They may start to mutter under their breath, fidget, complain of feeling hot, scribble on paper, or say they feel ill. See if the child or teacher can recognise these signs.

- If anger is an issue at school, work with the school to raise the awareness of teaching and support staff. It is essential that staff do not inadvertently aggravate the situation. Discuss the possibility of a time-out card for the child, so that they can go somewhere safe and quiet to calm themselves down.

- Teach the child simple distraction techniques to use when they begin to get irritated. Perhaps counting backwards from fifty/thirty/twenty. Something that is not complicated, but hard enough for the child to need to concentrate. To have a simple poem or phase to repeat over and over in their head or imagine the person who is annoying them to be something ridiculous: a goldfish, a parrot, a warthog, or a frog.

- Explain to the child how to get involved in another activity when they feel they may be losing control; an activity that they enjoy and that is calming: colouring, going for a walk outside, listening to music, or playing a computer game.

- Turn anger and frustration into action or physical work. Encourage them to do something energetic to burn off pent-up anger: kick a ball against a wall, run around the garden, skip on the spot, or go for a bike ride. Anything that will leave them physically tired. If the activity is useful, all the better: polish the family's shoes, shred school paper, mow the lawn, or hoover their bedroom.

- Practise relaxation techniques. There are numerous free apps that can be downloaded from the internet that use yoga, mindfulness, or meditation techniques.

- Explain that it can be useful to put yourself in the shoes of the other person when dealing with any aggravating behaviour. When others are unpleasant or mean, it will be because of some problem they have. They may be jealous, insecure, unhappy, ill, hungry, tired, or worried about something that you are unaware of.

- Sports such as martial arts will help with development of self-control.

- Persuade the child to step back and see events as they really are, rather than how they think they are. Identify any specific difficulties, talk about them and come up with options for dealing with the situation. Sharing problems and discussing them with others may help the child to see situations in a different light.

- Encourage the child to be stoical and accept that everyone will say thoughtless or hurtful things sometimes. The other person may not have meant what they said in the way it was interpreted, or perhaps they didn't have time to think about what they were saying, and how it might come across to the other person.

- Other children may target the child because they know they will get a reaction. Teach the child to ignore any goading behaviour, steer clear of bullies, stay close to adults or older children, and socialise with kinder peers.

- As a parent, try to model empathic behaviour yourself. Be seen to remain calm under stress, settle disputes within the family amicably and avoid confrontation. When an adult loses control, it will only add to the child's anxiety.

e. The child with sensory issues

Some children's nervous systems process physical stimuli inefficiently. They may not always recognise the sensations of being cold, hot, thirsty, or hungry.

Common signs of sensory processing issues:

- The child may react adversely to certain clothing, with some fabrics feeling too uncomfortable for the child to tolerate. Clothes may appear itchy or tight, with a tie making the child feel that they are being choked, or socks making the child feel they have pieces of cardboard in their shoes. The children will prefer loose, soft, and seamless garments with all of the labels removed: jogging bottoms, T shirts, polo shirts, and baggy sweatshirts.

- The child may have an intolerance to noise. Some children will be panicked by vacuum cleaners, hand-dryers, or sirens, with such sounds feeling like a physical pain. The child's reaction may be particularly extreme if the noise is unexpected.

- Over- or under-responding to the environment. Things that should cause discomfort, for example, being too hot or too cold, may provoke little reaction from the child. They may refuse to wear a coat or socks, even when it is snowing.

- Food textures and colours cause an exaggerated response. Food may have to be dry and light beige in colour, with anything that the child perceives as 'sloppy' making them physically gag. Meals have to be presented in a certain way, or they will be rejected; white toast always made from the same brand of bread, with all crusts removed, covered sparingly with one specific brand of spread. Children with sensory processing issues will often have an extremely limited diet.

These children require calm reassurance that carers understand their problems, take their concerns seriously, and are willing, (and able), to provide solutions. The situation for most children will improve as they get older, their nervous systems mature, and they gain more life experience.

f. ASC and special interests

One characteristic of Autistic Spectrum Condition is the pursuit of particular interests, often in a compulsive way. Typical interests would include:

<u>Science and fantasy fiction.</u> Depending on their ability level, children may learn every detail of a particular universe, write their own stories, watch the same films over and over again, or collect specific comics and magazines.

<u>Engineering and mechanical interests</u>. Many children excel at taking apart and re-building devices ranging from alarm clocks to small engines.

<u>Gaming</u>. Games come in many levels of difficulty and complexity and have a special appeal because of their technical challenge and logical and rule-based format. All players must adhere to the rules with no 'interpretation' allowed.

<u>Lego</u>. Lego is very popular with younger children, with more complex material and Lego Technik for the older individual. An interest in Lego can be pursued in many ways in addition to building the models: visiting Legoland, Lego films, conventions, clubs, and exhibitions.

<u>Trains</u>. Train spotting is a time-honoured male activity, and there are masses of options available for the train enthusiast to pursue their hobby: train museums, Thomas the Tank Engine TV programmes and associated merchandise, train-related videos and books, model train layouts, or joining railway modelling clubs.

Involving themselves in an 'obsessive' interest is one way in which children can safely de-stress, (although there can be a danger of the interest becoming all-consuming). Some children are fortunate enough to be able to turn their lifelong hobby into a satisfying career.

Greta Thunberg has spoken about being on the ASC spectrum, and some of the benefits ASC has provided. As a result of her single-minded focus and tenacity, she has taken on World leaders, and spoken eloquently at the United Nations and the World Economic Forum about Global Warming, her 'obsessive' interest.

CHAPTER 4

HELPING CHILDREN TO LEARN

INTRODUCTION

The term <u>metacognition</u> means <u>learning how to learn</u>. Some children acquire the skills necessary for learning in an instinctive way, while other children find such skills less intuitive.

Study skills come under the umbrella of metacognitive skills and describe those methods and approaches to study used by successful individuals. Such approaches would include an understanding of how to: write different types of essays, give oral presentations, work in groups, revise for tests and exams, organise work, take accurate notes, read and spell at an appropriate level, and concentrate in lessons.

Study Skills are useful for everyone, but not every child will acquire them incidentally, and so they are a valuable addition to the curriculum, either as a discreet subject, or embedded within mainstream classes.

1. METACOGNITION

a. What is metacognition?

The expression 'metacognition' means 'learning how to learn'.

When discussing metacognition, it is useful for children to be aware of the differences between individual brains. They will then be more aware of how their own brain works, and of how to play to their strengths, while supporting any personal weaknesses.

To help your child with metacognition:

➤ Encourage the child to think about how they learn. What are they good at? What do they find easy, and what is more difficult for them? Why might that be? What could they do to help themselves?

➤ Explain that the rate of brain maturation varies between individuals, so the children should focus on improving their own performance, and not worry about the progress of others.

➤ Help the child to develop skills. Rather than say, 'Why can't you learn these French/German/Spanish verbs?', work with them to find ways of learning foreign vocabulary. When children feel they possess some of the skills required to complete a task, their confidence will improve.

➤ Explain that they have choices. Would they find it easier to revise for a test first thing in the morning, to use websites for over-learning, study at a friend's house, or go to subject surgeries at school? If they have some control over the situation and are able to work in a way they prefer, they will be more motivated. Encourage them to take responsibility for their own learning, and express confidence in their choices.

➤ Remember that every child is different. Some children like to work in silence, while others find it hard to concentrate without background noise. Some children like a competitive atmosphere, while competition makes others nervous. One child may prefer to work in short bursts, while another will be able to work for longer periods of time.

➤ A healthy lifestyle is essential for learning. Explain to the child that adequate sleep, exercise, and a good diet all help the brain to work efficiently.

b. A 'How I Learn' questionnaire

This questionnaire can be used to develop a child's understanding of their personal strengths and weaknesses, and how to use this knowledge to help themselves. (Fictious responses are in italics.)

1. What do you enjoy most in school/outside school and why?

   I enjoy any sort of sport. I play for school and club hockey teams.

   I like Biology and English this year, because I like the teachers and I think they like me.

   Our English teacher lets us act out some of the set texts we're doing in class. That is good fun and helps me to understand what's going on in the story.

2. What do you find difficult in school and why?

   I find it really hard to revise for tests, especially in Maths. Mainly it's the wordy problems that confuse me.

   I'm OK at most subjects in class, but sometimes I can't get my ideas down on paper properly. I need five good GCSEs to get into college and I'm not sure I'll get them.

3. How would you describe your favourite teachers? What aspect of their teaching do you find useful?

   Our Geography teacher is good because she explains things clearly. We watch YouTube clips and use the computer a lot in her lessons, which is much more interesting than just listening to her talking.

   I like teachers who let you ask questions without getting cross. They have a bit of a sense of humour but can keep control of the class. A relaxed, but fairly quiet atmosphere helps me to learn, I get distracted if it gets too noisy.

4. What type of lessons do you <u>not</u> enjoy or learn from?

   I find it hard to concentrate when teachers talk for a long time, and you have to sit and listen. I lose concentration. Then they won't let you ask questions. They say they've already told you something, but they haven't.

5. Is there anything you would like to change about yourself?

   I'm good at sport and drama, and I've got lots of friends, so I'm mostly happy with myself. I sometimes wish I could do better in tests and exams. I'm usually disappointed by my results.

6. Do you know how you learn best?

   I like doing practical things like experiments in Physics and Chemistry, to help me to understand things better. I like it when the teacher gives you lots of everyday examples, so you can see how the theory applies in the real world. I find it helpful to work with a partner; sometimes they can explain things in a different way, or you can explain stuff to them. I enjoy using IT because it helps me to concentrate.

7. If you were to design a new school with different ways of teaching and learning, what would it be like?

   I'd have a lot more sport, some type of sport every day. I could concentrate more in the boring lessons if I knew I had a Games or PE lesson next.

   I'd have more choice of practical subjects, like: Photography, Drama, Dance, Food Technology, or Design Technology.

2. LANGUAGE AND UNDERSTANDING

a. Receptive and expressive language

Receptive language refers to the language that the child *understands*. For example, the words that people use in conversation and the meaning behind what they say, or the vocabulary and information that the child reads. Most children's level of receptive language will be above their level of expressive language.

Expressive language refers to the language that the child *uses*. How they put their thoughts into words and sentences in a way that makes sense and is grammatically accurate.

b. Extending children's vocabulary

There is a direct link between educational success and the size of a child's vocabulary.

Facts about the acquisition of vocabulary.

- ✓ By Year 3 some children will have a vocabulary of 3,000 words and others 7,000 words.
- ✓ Children between the ages of one and twelve learn between 2.2 and 2.4 new words every day.
- ✓ By the time they enter Senior School, a child will need a vocabulary of 9,000 words to cope academically.
- ✓ 25% of the adult population have a vocabulary of between 6,000 and 12,000 words.
- ✓ 18-year olds in full-time education will have a vocabulary of between 12,000 and 18,000 words.
- ✓ The majority of university graduates will have a vocabulary of

between 18,000 and 24,000 words.

When a child has a good vocabulary, it will be easier for them to understand what is going on in the classroom and what the teacher is talking about. They will find it easier to maintain concentration in lessons, to follow instructions, to understand written texts, and to participate in class discussion.

Vocabulary plays an essential part in comprehension. A young child who is beginning to learn to read would sound a word out letter by letter: c-a-t, but if the child did not know what a cat was, they would not understand what they were reading. It is easy for teachers to think a child has understood a text because they have 'read' the words, but even the most intelligent person is capable of barking at print. It is possible to decode the words of a French text with a smattering of the language but have absolutely no understanding of the content.

As children move through school, they may appear articulate, but only be using conversational language, and have little understanding of the formal words used in written material. This will put them at a distinct disadvantage in secondary school. The most effective way for individuals to increase their formal vocabulary is through reading. This would be an example of the Matthew Effect or, 'To those that have, shall be given more'. If a child is a good reader, they will enjoy reading and so read more. This in turn will improve their vocabulary and their reading skills.

c. Idioms and proverbs

Higher order language skills include understanding inference. Idioms and proverbs will provide valuable practice for the child in recognising inference, or 'reading between the lines.'

Popular proverbs include:

1. Practice makes perfect. *(If you want to do something well, you need to put in the necessary effort in order to improve.)*

2. Two heads are better than one. *(If you work with others, you will be more likely to find a solution.)*

3. Better late than never. *(It is preferable for someone to arrive or do something late, rather than not at all.)*

4. The early bird catches the worm. *(The person who arrives first will have the best chance of success.)*

5. The devil makes work for idle hands. *(If individuals have nothing to do, they will get up to mischief.)*

6. Every cloud has a silver lining. *(Disappointment often comes with some compensation.)*

7. Birds of a feather, flock together. *(Individuals gravitate towards like-minded people.)*

8. Time flies when you're enjoying yourself. *(Time passes quickly when you're having fun.)*

9. It never rains but it pours. *(When something goes wrong, everything seems to go wrong.)*

10. Don't count your chickens before they are hatched. *(Don't assume anything too soon.)*

11. Beauty is in the eye of the beholder. *(Everyone has different opinions about who or what is attractive.)*

12. A stitch in time saves nine. *(If you do something straight away, it is certain to save time in the long run.)*

d. Increasing children's general knowledge

Sometimes even though a child can decode the words of a text, they will have limited comprehension because of poor general knowledge.

The sentence, 'The cat sat on the mat', would be difficult to understand if a reader was uncertain of what a cat or a mat was, and how the domesticated animal from the cat family tends to live in the family home.

Teachers can make assumptions about pupil's background knowledge that will present difficulties for the children throughout their education.

Impoverished general knowledge will increase a child's difficulty when the focus of reading moves from decoding (sounding words out), to reading for understanding. It is easy to assume that when a child can read a passage, they can understand it, but comprehension is rarely at the same level as decoding.

One of the main ways in which general knowledge can be increased is through reading, and so once again the weak reader is placed at a disadvantage. If a child can be persuaded to read non-fiction, they will acquire a broad knowledge of a range of topics. Non-fiction material can appeal to the less motivated reader because the written text will be supported by pictures, diagrams, charts, and photos.

To extend children's general knowledge:

- Select and read newspaper or magazine articles that you know will interest the child.

- Encourage curiosity through modelling.

  'I wonder why that happened? Just a moment and I'll look it up and see who was involved.'

- Help the child to research information. Why are there five rings in the Olympic symbol? Why are the rings different colours? Why are they those colours? Who designed that symbol and when? Get the children into the habit of finding answers, rather than simply being curious, but then moving on.

- Use personal interests to develop general knowledge. If the reader supports Chelsea Football Club, their interest could generate curiosity about the club's geographical whereabouts, its history, the country of origin of any international players, match statistics, how injuries will affect the players, the cost of players, and footballers' salaries compared to those of other occupations.

e. A General Knowledge Quiz (Secondary school children)

1. What is another word for the low ground between two hills?
2. Who was Neil Armstrong?
3. What is a song for two called?
4. What name is given to a young kangaroo?
5. Who was Edward Jenner?
6. What is another word for an enclosure that contains birds?
7. What is the common name for the spine?
8. Who ran the first mile in under four minutes?
9. Give an example of an idiom
10. What do we call a field where fruit trees are grown?
11. Who wrote 'A Christmas Carol'?
12. What do we call the meat of a deer?
13. What is another word for the steps on a ladder?
14. Who is credited with the invention of television?
15. What is another word for a fertile place in the desert?
16. Who was Rodin?
17. Who was Horatio Nelson?
18. What does the acronym RSVP mean?
19. Who was Margaret Thatcher?

20. What is another word for a substance used to counteract poisoning, for example, in a snake bite?

21. What is another name for a place where fish are kept?

22. Who was Long John Silver?

23. What is another word for shallow crossing in a river?

24. What is another word for the shiny material that is often used to make wedding dresses?

(If you don't know the answers, look them up.)

3. READING

a. What are phonics?

Children are neurologically capable of learning to read between the ages of five and seven years, with boys ready to learn slightly later on average than girls. Individual children will develop at different rates, and it is important not to make the late bloomer feel anxious about their level of competence. Similarly, there is no point in accelerating the early developer, if in a few years' time the child's pleasure in reading has been crushed by constant exposure to 'challenging' material.

Currently in schools, children are taught to read using phonics. This approach focuses on the links between letters and sounds. When the child can remember these letter – sound links – they will be able to sound words out: c – a – t for cat, s – u – n for sun. This process is known as decoding. The first reading books the children are given will contain simple words that can be sounded out easily: fat, cap, sit, pen and run.

Warning. There are 26 letters in the English alphabet that make up 44 speech sounds called phonemes. Each speech sound or phoneme has a written equivalent as below.

I take it you already know

Of tough and bough and cough and dough?

Others may stumble, but not you,

On hiccough, thorough, lough and through?

Well done! And now you wish, perhaps,

To learn of less familiar traps?

Beware of heard, a dreadful word

That looks like beard and sounds like bird,

And dead: it's said like bed, not bead –

For goodness sake don't call it deed!

Watch out for meat and great and threat

(They rhyme with suite and straight and debt).

A moth is not a moth in mother,

Nor both in bother, broth in brother,

And here is not a match for there

Nor dear and fear for bear and pear,

And then there's dose and rose and lose –

Just look them up – and goose and choose,

And cork and work and card and ward,

And font and front and word and sword,

And do and go and thwart and cart –

Come, come, I've hardly made a start!

A dreadful language? Man alive!

I'd mastered it when I was five!

(Richard Krogh.)

As can be seen, English is not a phonetically regular language because it has roots in many other languages: Latin, French, German, Italian, Spanish, Dutch, Scandinavian, Japanese, Arabic, Irish, and Yiddish. As a result, there are innumerable words that follow different sets of phonetic rules and, even in the early stages of learning to read, pupils will need to recognise common, but phonetically irregular, keywords such as: there, said, was, they, come, so, here, and does.

Twelve of these keywords make up a quarter of everything that we read and write. A hundred of the keywords make up half of everything that we read and write, so it is essential that a child recognises these commonly used words if their reading is to be fluent.

Some children may be more suited to learning to read through a keyword approach. This method is called the 'Look and Say' method of teaching reading. Initially, children taught in this way will read simple books containing a few keywords, then gradually, as they learn more keywords, the number of words in each book is increased. This approach may suit children with a visual learning style, and a good visual, rather than auditory, memory.

b. Hearing a child read

Every reader's level of skill will improve with regular practice. Children become readers by reading.

Ensure your child sees you reading regularly: newspapers, emails, manuals, recipes, magazines, books, notices, post cards, food labels, and instructions; anything that stresses the importance of reading in everyday life.

When hearing children read:

- Discuss the title and look at a few of the pictures in the book before starting to read. This will set the scene and help the child make sense of the text.

- Whilst reading, read parts of the text yourself to keep momentum going: a sentence, a paragraph, or a page depending on the child's fluency and motivation. When you read, if you make an error, correct yourself naturally and then move on. This will show the child that no-one reads perfectly, and that making a few errors isn't anything to be concerned about.

- Watch the child and mimic any useful behaviour, for example, if they track the text with their finger, you do the same. If they frequently lose their place on the page, put a piece of card under the line they are reading. When they have read that line, they can move the card down below the next line of print.

- Ignore any minor errors which do not change the meaning of a passage. It isn't much fun for the child to feel their reading is expected to be perfect.

- Draw the child's attention to any illustrations. Pictures will help them to understand the text by providing a visual overview of the action.

- If the child gets stuck, prompt them. If they are making numerous errors and their reading is becoming laborious, always give the word immediately. As a rule of thumb, if the child cannot recognise or easily decode five words on any one page, the text will be too frustrating for them to read.

- Children are all different, and there is no one right way to teach a child to read. If adults explain how they tackle words they cannot identify immediately, the child will learn alternative tactics. All strategies are legitimate. <u>There is no one secret way or single correct formula to teach children to read.</u>

- Be confident in using common sense approaches with material, for example, if a story has several characters with names that the child is finding hard to pronounce, call the characters by an easier alternative: Stanley Kowalski becomes Stan, and Viscount Raoul de Chagny becomes Rog.

- Give the child a choice of reading material. Sometimes they will want to tackle something wordy and at other times will prefer to read something straightforward. Comics, blogs, recipes, instruction manuals, road signs, football programmes, shopping lists, newspapers, internet sites, and menus will all provide reading practice and emphasise the point that reading is a useful life skill.

<u>c. Reading comprehension</u>

Reading comprehension means different things to different people. It may be considered a life skill, or an isolated exercise to be carried out in English lessons. Unfortunately, isolated exercises will only test a child's comprehension, rather than develop their skills.

Decoding is the basis of learning to read, but the primary purpose of reading is to understand. Good readers constantly monitor their understanding of what they read. They decide whether it is necessary to read all of the material carefully or to skim for general meaning. As they read, they judge whether or not they have really understood the passage, and whether this matters. Should they re-read, perhaps looking up a few unfamiliar words, or would they be better reading on and hoping there is a visual display of the information? Perhaps they need to stop reading, think about the material and try to put it into their own words?

Such strategies might not be obvious to weaker readers, who may assume that it is normal not to understand what you read. For some children reading is a difficult and rather pointless activity, to be done in isolation and of little relevance to anything else in their life.

To help develop a child's reading comprehension

- Take time before starting to read a text to talk about the background to the story and discuss any unfamiliar vocabulary. If the book is about Robin Hood, the child would need to know a little about when and where the story is set: what is Sherwood Forest, who was the Sheriff of Nottingham, why he hated Robin Hood, and the meaning of such words as: venison, longbow, friar, knight, monastery, and Norman.

- Encourage the child to predict what will happen next. Interaction with the story will help to reinforce the idea that the text should make sense.

- Encourage the child to develop their visualisation techniques. Visualisation is the process whereby the child changes the words of the passage into their own mental video, recreating the story visually in their minds. Whilst reading, ask the child a few questions about their video: What colour is your knight's horse? What time of year is it in your video? What does Maid Marion's dress look like?

- After reading a chapter, discuss the plot, characters, or events. Why did those things happen? Why did the characters behave in that way? What does the child think will happen next? This does not have to be an inquisition, just a casual conversation. Encourage the child to make sense of the action in the light of their own experience, and to relate the story to their own lives.

Would they have done what the main character did? If not, why not? What would you, as the adult, have done and why?

d. Measuring the KS3/KS4 child's reading speed

Use the child's set English text to work out their reading speed for reading aloud and reading silently. (A set text will be at the expected reading level of a child of their age.)

1. Ask the child to read aloud for two minutes. Put a pencil mark against their starting point and finishing point in the book

2. Count the number of words in any section of six lines of the text.

3. Divide the total number of words counted by six to get an average number of words per line.

4. Multiply the average number of words per line by the number of lines the child has read.

5. Halve this number to get a 'per minute' reading speed.

6. Repeat the process for silent reading.

If the scores for reading aloud and reading silently are the same, the child will be reading word for word when reading silently and will be at a disadvantage. Children in secondary school need two reading speeds; slower when reading aloud to decode and give appropriate emphasis to their reading, but quicker when reading silently to ensure that quantities of material can be read at a reasonable pace.

Ask the child to record their silent reading speed in this way each day for a week. The child can then read every day, focusing on reading at a slightly faster rate. At the end of the week, look together at their daily record to see how much they have improved with effort and targeted practice. (Hint: Ask the child a few simple questions about the text to discourage any cheating!)

If the child practices with simple texts initially, the vocabulary and content will be straight forward, and poor comprehension of the text will not detract from the overall aim of increasing reading speed.

e. Increasing silent reading speed

There is a balance to be struck between reading quickly and processing information accurately. It would be pointless for a child to read at a fast pace, but with no understanding.

Improving reading speed is really a question of reading more effectively.

To increase a child's silent reading speed:

- The reader must pay attention. Turn off the television, radio, and mobile phone.

- It is easier to focus for a certain amount of time: ten minutes concentrated reading without stopping, then take a break.

- Check that the light is adequate before starting to read. Reading is more of an effort if the child has to strain their eyes.

- If the child is squinting, or holding books close to their eyes, book an eye test for them.

- Encourage the child to keep their eyes moving from left to right steadily across the page, and to avoid re-reading the text. The brain will become accustomed to filling in any gaps. To help the child maintain a steady speed, use a ruler as a tracking tool. Keep the ruler below the line being read and move the ruler down the page steadily, so that the eyes are forced to keep pace.

- Encourage the child to use the punctuation of a text to read blocks of words, rather than read every word separately.

- When reading silently, chewing gum or sucking a sweet may be enough to stop the reader from sub-vocalising (whispering the words one by one as if reading aloud).

- Show the child how to use different reading techniques for different purposes. For example, skimming passages to get the overall meaning of a text. Skimming involves looking at pictures and diagrams, reading introductions, conclusions, summaries, or headings. It may become obvious to the child that they don't need to read the whole chapter, but just, for example, the section on imports and exports, which has a clear pie graph to summarise the written text.

- Experiment with different coloured overlays to try to reduce any visual discomfort. These can be made by cutting A4 coloured plastic sheets in half. If the child lays the sheet over the page they are reading, the contrast between page and print will be reduced, making reading a more comfortable experience. These coloured A4 sheets can be bought at all High Street stationery shops.

- Unfamiliar vocabulary will slow a child's reading down. It may be worth the child targeting words from specific subjects. If they find Biology texts challenging, try to make sure they know the meaning of any unusual biological words.

f. Different Reading Techniques

One way in which children can increase their reading speed is to read more efficiently. When looking for information about lions' eating habits, it would be pointless to read a whole book about lions. If the child is looking for the time of the next bus home, it would be a mistake to read the timetable from beginning to end. This may seem glaringly obvious to an adult but is not always apparent to a child.

There are three recognised approaches a child can take when reading for information: skimming, scanning, and close reading.

1.   <u>Skimming.</u> Skimming involves looking at a book or part of a book, to see if it contains the information needed. No reading is required: the child flicks through the pages, looking at titles, chapter headings, summaries, diagrams, and illustrations.

2.   <u>Scanning.</u> Scanning is the method used when seeking specific information: the time of a train, a phone number, the date of a concert, information about transpiration, volcanoes, or greenhouse gases. The child will need to understand how to use an index, chapter headings, summaries, glossaries, and tables to access specific information quickly.

3.   <u>Close reading.</u> Close reading involves careful reading, word for word, in order to understand the text. This can be difficult for children who have little interest in a topic. It will be easy for them to drift off, lose concentration, and find they have 'read' several pages, but cannot remember a single word. Most secondary children will be taking a range of subjects in Key Stage 3 and 4, and a lack of intrinsic interest in some topics is inevitable. If they are to maintain concentration, the child will need to read actively. They may claim that they have read the material, but can't seem to take anything in. Explain that they should do something whilst reading, for example:

✓ Read the passage aloud and stop at the end of each page to summarise mentally what they have read or note down a few key words or points from the page.

✓ Highlight or underlines specific parts of the text in different colours: names in blue, dates in red, countries in green, or subject keywords in orange.

✓ Make a visual summary of the text: a comic strip, diagram, graph, timeline, or a mind map.

✓ An adult could read the text aloud, and the child retell the gist of the passage in their own words.

g. Motivating the reluctant reader

When encouraging the reluctant reader, always provide a choice of material. All reading is good. Do not be tempted to direct the child towards worthy material but respect their preferences and start from their personal interests. Children who find reading a chore may have been asked to read books beyond their capability and, if the material has bored them, the whole activity will have seemed painfully pointless. It is quite acceptable to pick up a book and not read past the first few pages because it doesn't interest you. Just because Grandma bought you 'War and Peace' for Christmas does not mean you have to read it.

Personal interest is an essential aspect of reading motivation. Many children imagine fiction books to be the only proper books and an introduction to other genres of texts and confirmation of their importance as reading material, can be a revelation. Magazines, websites, newspaper articles, annuals, poetry, manuals, song lyrics, comics, and puzzle books would all fall into this non-fiction category. Newspaper articles about topics of interest, for example: art, TV celebrities, music, politics, gaming, sport, animals, environmental issues, films, fashion, and current affairs will all provide interesting reading material. There will be a magazine or comic that links to every interest or hobby a child could possibly have. This kind of non-fiction material can be browsed through; the child doesn't need to read the text sequentially from beginning to end.

As the aim is to motivate the child to read, it doesn't matter whether the chosen material will provide challenge, extension, or reading development opportunities. When the reading relates to a child's interests, it is surprising how much their understanding and knowledge of the topic will improve their reading fluency. A keen horse rider will not stumble over such words as equestrian, whinny, thoroughbred, pedigree, and martingale. They will be able to recognise the words and understand what they mean. However, if the same child were reading a passage at a similar level that included specialist baseball terminology, they would be able to read very little and understand even less.

Collections of short stories can be appealing to readers with limited reading stamina. Some stories will be short enough to read in one sitting and condensed enough for the reader with a memory weakness to understand without the need to re-read.

Comic books or Manga texts will give children valuable visual input to support their reading of the printed text, in addition to being acceptable material in the eyes of their peers.

Sometimes an introduction to a specific author or series of books can be a motivator. If an adult or good reader reads sections of a text aloud, the child may be interested enough to read on, and then to seek out other books by that author, or books from the same series.

All forms of reading are valid: iPads, kindles, websites, books online, and blogs. It is surprising how many children feel that listening to a set text on a tablet is somehow not allowed. This demonstrates what a negative experience reading must be for some children; if they are not struggling and frustrated, they must be cheating.

Associations such as the United Kingdom Literacy Association, the School Library Association, and the National Literacy Trust are an excellent source of resources and ideas for promoting reading across different ages.

4. SPELLING

a. The development of spelling

Spelling follows the same developmental pattern in every child.

There are several models of spelling development, some more complicated than others. The basic model consists of four stages: logographic, alphabetic, phonological, and automatic.

Stage 1. Logographic. This is the stage a child reaches when they put pen to paper for the first time. They will try to draw visual graphics such as the McDonalds or British Rail logo, traffic signs, or symbols from TV programmes.

Stage 2. Alphabetic. At this stage the child links their spelling attempts to letters and sounds. At first children only note down the beginning and ending sounds of a word, for example: ME = Mummy.

Stage 3. Phonological. Although the child's spelling at this stage is not accurate, the attempts at words would be easily understood with all sounds represented by a letter: 'n-I-t' for night, 's-u-m' for some and s-e-d' for said.

Stage 4. Automatic. This stage is reached when a correct spelling is recalled automatically, allowing the child to write fluently and to concentrate on the content of their work, rather than their spelling.

As adults we will move between stages when we are uncertain of the spelling of a word. We write the word down as we sound it out phonetically, perhaps doing this several times and comparing the spellings to see which alternative looks correct.

b. Helping your child with spelling

Many children will have no idea of how to learn spellings. Experiment with a few different strategies to see which they find most useful.

1. Use word families. Would, should, could. Fright, might, tonight, bright, and fight.

2. Over-pronounce the word to draw attention to letters that are not stressed in speech. Arctic not Ar/tic, environment not enviro/ment.

3. Write the spelling out several times to try to remember the way the word 'feels' when written.

4. Look for common roots in spellings. 'Cent' meaning one hundred, as in century, centipede and centurion, therefore, centimetre cannot be sentimetre, because it is related to a hundred.

5. Learn some basic spelling rules: 'i' before 'e' except after 'c'.

6. To avoid the danger of the child shortening the spelling, pronounce each syllable in the word: choc / o / late (chocolate), rather than choc / late.

7. Be aware of suffixes and prefixes: appoint, appointed, disappoint, disappointing, disappointment.

8. Write the word several times in different coloured pens, saying each letter name aloud: E-G-Y-P-T. E-G-Y-P-T. E-G-Y-P-T.

9. Look for words within words: 'spit' in hospital, 'secret' in secretary.

10. For any tricky spelling that the child finds particularly hard, try the following routine. Copy the word out correctly, look closely at the word, saying each letter aloud, then cover the word over and write it out in capital letters. Check you have spelt the word correctly, then cover it over again. Write the word out with the hand you do

not usually use for writing, then check back to make sure you have spelt it correctly. Cover the word over again, and then write it out in bubble writing, then check you have spelt it correctly. Think of two other words that have a similar meaning. Look at the word again, then shut your eyes, and say the letters in the word aloud, working from the last letter to the first.

Using a variety of approaches as above will ensure the child is looking carefully at the word, and registering the individual letters and the order in which they occur.

11. Record the correct spellings of any frequent errors in a notebook. Keep the notebook somewhere handy, perhaps in the front pocket of a school bag or blazer.

12. Use mnemonics. These can be pictures or little sayings. Some common mnemonics take the letters of the word in their correct order, and make them into a sentence, for example: 'big elephants can always understand small elephants' (because), or 'rhythm has your two hips moving' (rhythm).

My pupils always enjoy competitions to create attractive or amusing mnemonic posters for spellings they find hard. On one occasion I failed to give clear instructions and a sweet little seven-year-old girl found a very hard word herself in the dictionary and devised a clever mnemonic with accompanying picture. 'Hattie And Emily Mouse Ordered Roger Rabbit's Horse Ollie In Doors ... at least I knew her parents hadn't helped her.

c. Twenty mnemonics

<u>Separate</u> = You can't se-**para**-te a **para** from his chute.

<u>Accommodation</u> = The a-**cc**-o-**mm**-odation has **2 c** /ots and **2 m** /attresses.

<u>Father</u> = **Fat - her**

<u>Accident</u> = When **C**ars **C**ollide, they make a **Dent**.

<u>Friend</u> = I will be your fri-**end** until the **end**.

<u>Caribbean</u> = A carib **/** bean

<u>Special</u> = The **CIA** are spe-**cia**-l agents.

<u>Hear</u> = I h-**ear** with my **ear**

<u>Address</u> = Add your **add**-ress

<u>Rhythm</u> = **R**hythm **has your two hips m**oving.

<u>Secretary</u> = A **secret**ary can keep a **secret**.

<u>Parallel</u> = Parallel has 2 para-**ll**-el lines in the mi**dd**le.

<u>Stationery / stationary</u> = Station**e**ry includes **e**nvelopes. Station**a**ry at the train st**a**tion.

<u>Piece</u> = A **pie**-ce of pie.

<u>Believe</u> = Who would be-**lie**-ve a **lie**?

<u>Necessary</u> = It is ne**c**e**ss**ary for a shirt to have **one c** /ollar and **two s** /leeves.

<u>Because</u> = **B**ig **e**lephants **c**an **a**lways **u**nderstand **s**maller **e**lephants.

<u>Together</u> = To / get / her

<u>Island</u> = An island **is land** surrounded by water.

<u>Conscience</u> = **Con**– **science** is a science.

5. STUDY SKILLS

a. What are Study Skills?

'Study Skills' describe the methods and approaches to study used by successful pupils. These approaches would include an understanding of how to: write different types of essays, work in groups, revise for tests, manage their time, organise work, take accurate notes, read effectively, and concentrate in class.

These skills are essential for everyone, but not all children acquire them incidentally, and some will need to be taught them directly.

b. A Study Skills questionnaire

A questionnaire can explore a child's specific study skills strengths and weaknesses and provide a basis for discussion about any areas that require development.

1. Reading

➤ Do you read for pleasure? What sort of reading material do you choose?

➤ When reading silently, do you read slowly word for word?

➤ Do you use different ways of reading in different circumstances?

➤ Do you have enough time to complete reading tasks set in class or for homework?

2. Memory

➤ What techniques do you use when revising for tests and exams?

➤ Do you find it easy to remember French/German/Spanish

vocabulary, and scientific and mathematical formulae?

➤ Can you remember sequences easily, for example, times tables?

3. Attention.

➤ Can you listen throughout a lesson, or does your attention wander?

➤ If you do lose concentration in a lesson, what do you do?

➤ Do you always participate fully in class?

➤ When you are asked a question or to repeat instructions, are you always able to remember what has been said?

4. Organisation.

➤ Do you regularly forget or lose equipment, homework, and sports kit?

➤ Is your desk/bedroom/locker/schoolbag tidy?

➤ Can you always locate your possessions?

5. Note-taking.

➤ Do you find it easy to pick out the important facts from information?

➤ How do you take notes? (Write everything down? Record information in bullet points? Mind map?)

➤ Can you take notes while listening to the teacher talking?

6. Essays.

➤ Do you always understand what an essay title is asking you to do?

➤ Do you have a problem with planning essays? Do you know what to include and what to leave out?

➤ Do you have a good grasp of basic grammar and punctuation?

➤ Are you aware of the strengths and weaknesses that teachers regularly identify in your essays?

7. Spelling.

➤ Has spelling ever been a problem for you?

➤ Do you use spellcheckers?

➤ Do you always proofread your work?

8. Presentation of work.

➤ Is your handwriting legible?

➤ Are your diagrams and drawings neat?

➤ Can you write quickly enough to complete tasks within the allotted time?

➤ Are you ever disappointed with the appearance of your work?

9. Exams and revision.

➤ Do you find revision difficult? What aspect do you find most difficult?

➤ Are the grades you get in exams similar to the grades you get for class work?

➤ Do your exam results reflect the effort you make to revise?

➤ Do you get unduly anxious about exams?

10. Group work and oral presentations.

➤ Are you able to give confident oral presentations?

➤ Can you work as a member of a group?

➤ Do you enjoy group work?

c. Organised people are too idle to look for things

Organisation can become more of a problem for children when they move from junior to senior school. In senior school pupils will be expected to organise themselves and manage independently throughout the school day.

The best time to discuss the need for good organisation is when the children are starting secondary school, when they will be more motivated to act upon advice.

Advice for children.

- Keep a spare set of equipment in several places: schoolbag, class locker, and at home. Transparent pencil cases are useful as the contents are always visible. You will be able to see instantly if you have left your compasses at home and need to borrow a pair.

- Make a 'to do' list and review the list daily; perhaps keeping a white board in your bedroom to write the lists on. You can then note down work that is still outstanding, erase work you have completed, and record important dates: sport fixtures, friends' birthdays, and test times.

- Keep a notebook in your pocket or schoolbag to jot down anything of importance that you must remember.

- Keep a few spare timetables at school and at home.

- If your subject files are colour coded; perhaps green for Maths, blue for English, and red for Science, you will be more likely to pick up the correct file even if you are in a hurry or distracted.

- Make an index at the front of subject files for the topics you have covered in class and use coloured paper to separate notes from different topics. Keep sections at the back of the file for definitions and subject-specific spellings.

- Back up all computer work. It may be worth asking teaching staff if you can send your homework in electronically to save work being mislaid between home and school.

- Get into routines. If you always keep everything in the same place: trainers always in your locker; bus pass always in your jacket pocket; pencil case always in your schoolbag, your belongings and equipment are more likely to always be in the same place, even if you were not concentrating when you put them away.

- Pack your schoolbag each evening. Then there will be enough time to review tomorrow's timetable, find your swimming kit, borrow a sibling's calculator, or ask parents to complete permission slips. Spend a few minutes each week tidying your schoolbag and locker, throwing away any broken equipment or litter.

- Label everything: sports kit, books, and equipment, then, when things get lost, they should find their way back to you.

d. Time management

Children who experience a problem with time management may be able to tell the time but have little sense of the passage of time. They seem unable to estimate the amount of time necessary to complete a task, tending to leave everything until the last minute. They will aim to leave the house for school at 8.15 a.m. but fail to factor in the time necessary to dress and eat breakfast. They seem to have little idea of how long activities take, enthusiastically creating a 'to do' list for the day, without realising that the activities would in reality take a week or two to complete, particularly if procrastination is a problem for the child.

Conversely, when an activity is of personal interest, the child can become totally absorbed and unaware of how much time has passed.

Such behaviour will give adults the impression that the child is simply selecting if and when they choose to involve themselves.

To improve time management

o Ask the children when their most serious time management problems occur and discuss ways of dealing with these specific issues.

o Refer to the clock regularly to demonstrate how adults monitor the use of time.

o Set stop watches or timers for the amount of time the children should spend on a task.

o Use family calendars at home to record important dates: school holidays, dental appointments, or family celebrations. Refer to the calendar in front of the child. How many more days until the weekend? How long until Sports Day? How many weeks until the Christmas concert?

o Use estimates to give the child a feel for the passage of time. It takes approximately fifteen minutes for the bus to get into town, netball matches have exactly fifteen minutes per quarter, and it takes about fifteen minutes to walk home. Then use the same period of time for estimations. You know that one quarter of a netball match lasts for 15 minutes: you have the same length of time to get ready for Guides/judo practice/tea/to catch the bus.

o Ask the children to guess how long they think an activity will take to complete, and then to time themselves as they do the task. A stopwatch can turn a guessing game into a useful learning experience.

e. Time management. Advice for children

- Good time management is a question of being organised. Develop routines and habits. If you make a 'to do' list and look at it regularly, you will be more likely to manage your time effectively.

- Aim for a pragmatic approach rather than perfectionism. Target what must be done from your 'to do' list and do it. Do not ponder what could be done, that will waste time.

- Try to manage your workload in a steady, measured way. Break tasks down into small, achievable sections. 'I will start revising early for next week's test by making bullet point summaries of each topic for fifteen minutes each night. Only fifteen minutes per night, while Mum is watching the News.'

- It is important to realise that studying efficiently does not mean putting in more hours, but identifying what is essential, and then working on that. If you do something properly the first time, it is finished, and there will be no need to return to it, think about doing more, or change what you've done.

- Use timers on your phone or computer so you are working to the alarm, and less likely to allow yourself to be side tracked.

- When you are short of time for reading, read only what is relevant. Do not get bogged down by reading around the subject, go for the essentials.

- Use mobile phone alerts as reminders of timings or dates. If you have a tendency to always be late to meet friends, set your watch 15 minutes early, or apologise in advance, and ask the friends to send you reminder texts.

- Set SMART targets for yourself. SMART = Specific: I will read two pages of the book every night this week. Measurable: I will summarise what has happened on those pages and tell Mum at breakfast. Achievable: I will be able do the reading in the ten minutes before I go to bed. Realistic: I can fit this in, as it won't take me long. Timely: By reading two pages every night, I will have read a chapter by the weekend.

f. Motivation

There are two types of motivation: intrinsic motivation and extrinsic motivation.

Intrinsic motivation is when the child wants to be able to do something for their own personal satisfaction.

Extrinsic motivation occurs when children are motivated by external factors such as rewards, threats, praise, or punishment.

Helping a child to develop intrinsic motivation.

o The brain will take a calculated risk when considering an activity. How much effort will be required, and what will the benefits of that effort be. A child's motivation will decrease if they feel an activity is pointless, so help them to work out what is in it for them. What is their ultimate aim? Do they need a specific exam result? Do they want to prove a point?

o Motivation will decrease when a child feels forced to do an activity, so try to include choice in tasks. When they know they have a choice, the child will feel more in control. In school this choice could be how a piece of work is to be completed: a presentation made to peers, an essay, a short video, a quiz on the topic for the class, or an illustrated timeline.

o Everyone will work more enthusiastically at a task when they feel they have the necessary level of competence, so help the child to develop the necessary skills.

o Help them to manage their environment. They might find they are more productive if they work with a friend, in the garden, at a grandparent's house, or in the public library.

o Surround them with pleasant and positive people. Talking to supportive family members and friends will boost their confidence and encourage their work ethic.

o Help your child to see the big picture; to imagine what it will be like to finish a task, succeed at the challenge set, manage the demands made of them, and receive positive feedback.

o When they have doubts, remind them of previous successes. To think of other things that they have done well, and to tell themselves that, as they have succeeded before, they will be able to do so again.

o Try to establish short-term and long-term goals, so the child can take a small-step approach, whilst still being aware of their ultimate aims. If a setback occurs during a small-steps approach, any damage is easily rectified.

o The child should allow themselves rewards and incentives along the way or when they reach a personal goal. 'When I have finished a week of work experience, I'll buy that CD/go to the cinema/watch that box set.'

o Explain how the child can monitor their performance by keeping a list of tasks to be done and ticking each one off when completed to provide evidence of their progress.

o Encourage the child to have a go and always try to do their best. Emphasise that the only regrets they will have in the future will relate to things they didn't do, rather than the things they did do.

o Explain that they should get going on a task without waiting until they are ready. If they start work without any over-thinking, their brain will not have time to come up with excuses.

o Regular rewards will help a child to persist with tedious tasks. Teach them how to make deals with themselves. If I can work for 20 minutes/finish this essay/tidy my bedroom/read the first chapter, then I can watch 'EastEnders'/have a bath/eat a packet of crisps.

o Tell the child to pretend to be motivated. When other people assume that they are motivated, they are more likely to be supportive and enthusiastic too, which may be enough to galvanise the child into action.

o Help the child to look after themselves and maintain a healthy lifestyle. When they are physically fit, they will be mentally fit. They should take adequate amounts of exercise, eat a balanced diet, and get enough sleep. If they feel things are getting on top of them, tell them to do something they know will help them to relax: have a bath, watch a DVD, take the dog for a walk, or meet up with friends.

g. What is procrastination?

When activities seem unappealing or boring, perhaps putting away belongings, returning plates to the kitchen, or tidying a bedroom, it would be quite normal for most children and teenagers to use avoidance tactics. Some children will adopt the same attitude towards schoolwork, even when they are in secondary school and public exams loom on the horizon. They are aware that the work must be completed, but just don't seem able to get started. Their procrastination may come across as apathy or laziness, but many children can become genuinely overwhelmed by a situation and find it easier to do nothing.

Most children will lack the motivation to complete tasks that seem boring or a waste of time, but they will have enough of a work habit or self-discipline to force themselves to get going. The child with a problem with procrastination will be the child who always waits until the last minute before producing scrappy and inadequate work. They will claim to be motivated by impending deadlines, however, work produced at the last minute will never be as well thought through as work completed carefully and at a steady pace. The child who rushes will not have time to think about the task and explore the different options that will give a well-rounded response.

Children procrastinate for many reasons. *(Solutions are in italics.)*

➤ They worry that the work is beyond their capability.

Ask what part of the work appears too difficult. What help do they need?

➤ They feel their work has to be perfect.

Discourage black and white thinking. There is a lot of grey between disaster and perfection. Do they need reassurance that the work only has to be 'good enough'?

➤ They do not know what to do or where to start.

Would a simpler explanation help them to understand what the task involves?

Identify exactly what it is that the child has to do to save them going down too many blind alleys and wasting time.

➤ The rewards for procrastination are too appealing. 'If I don't do this revision, I can have a look at social media sites.

Try to focus their attention on the reward that completing the work will bring. If I can get this done tonight, I'll have Saturday afternoon free to go to the cinema/shopping/watch the football match.

➤ The task seems pointless, boring, and the child would rather be doing something else, anything else. Children who have a tendency to be impulsive will also have a tendency to procrastinate. The appeal of doing something fun now being too appealing to ignore.

Is there an aspect of the topic that might interest them or could they be persuaded that completing the work would be useful to them in the long term? What is in it for them?

h. Avoiding Procrastination. Advice for children.

- Just do something and get going with a task. Get some ideas down and tell yourself you will worry later about such things as spelling and grammar.

- Try to see something in the activity that will benefit you and keep reminding yourself of how it will be helpful:

  ✓ 'I need Maths to get on my college course. I'll make clear revision notes this afternoon in my free period.'

  ✓ 'This Biology homework will help me with revision for my First Aid test at Cadets.'

  ✓ 'We're going on holiday next week. I'll need to know about tsunamis in case one happens while we're away. I'll read this chapter tonight.'

- Don't strive for perfection. Strive for, 'good enough, and finished'.

- Be very specific in your aims and keep them manageable:

  ✓ 'I will start revising by learning ten specialist terms, their spellings and definitions for the population module tonight. I know most of them anyway.'

  ✓ 'I will read Chapter One tonight after tea. The whole chapter is only six pages long.'

  ✓ 'This afternoon I will make a list of the parts of speech with an example for each one, ready to learn for Monday's test. After the test, I'll put the notes in my file to use as revision in the end of year exams.'

- Break work down into sub-tasks. Choose one small task to do and just do it without over-thinking. If you divide your work into different sized tasks, it will be easy to pick off a few of the smaller ones. Then, even if you have delayed starting the harder work, you are still working and making overall progress.

- Set the alarm on your watch or phone for fifteen minutes, then work until the alarm goes off. No ifs, no buts. If your mind starts to wander, use self-talk to bring yourself back on task, 'Stop faffing about and keep writing, you have nearly finished this paragraph. Focus.'

  Talking aloud to yourself is a good self-regulating method, because it sounds as though someone is there with you telling you what to do. Saying to yourself, 'Just stop all this panicking, you can do it. Pick up your pen and write the date and the title, then we'll think of the first sentence', will be reassuring.

- Procrastinators are often put off by the enormity of the whole and over-think things. Don't think about the whole, just take your work one step at a time. You don't have to start to write an essay or report at the beginning. You can write the conclusion first, or choose one point that you understand really well, and write that paragraph to get you going.

- Use simple self-help strategies; for example, put post-it notes of tasks that must be completed on your bedroom wall, then take one post-it off the wall, do the task, and throw the post-it away. This will help you to feel in control and give you a sense of progress.

- If distracting thoughts interrupt you, write them down on a piece of paper to look at when you have a break, then get back to the work.

- Working in short bursts may seem more manageable and help you to stay motivated. Ten minutes work is preferable to none. You may become so involved in a task, that you want to finish a particular section, and work on beyond your allotted time.

- Timetable free time into your day. When you know you have allowed yourself some space to do nothing, you are more likely to keep working knowing that free time is on the horizon, when you'll be able to chat with friends, go to the shopping centre, watch TV, or browse the internet without feeling guilty.

- If you hate the idea of working in isolation in your room, organise study periods at friends' houses or in the school library. Then you can have company but work at the same time. Choose conscientious, hardworking friends to help you to keep on task. When others are working around you, you may be able to work for longer periods.

- Stay busy. Procrastination is more likely to occur when you have time to waste. If you are aware of limitations on your free time, you will be more likely to get on with work.

Anyone who has a hobby that requires self-discipline, for example, taking part in a sport or playing a musical instrument, will be likely to possess the self-control necessary to overcome procrastination. If you play hockey for your year, school, or a club, you will understand the need for self-discipline. If you are a member of a choir or band, you will know that you must practice regularly, even when you don't want to. You will be aware of how to improve through a small-step approach and know that you feel good when a target has been achieved. You will understand the need to remain focused throughout routine practices.

Try taking up a hobby that provides you with opportunities for relaxation alongside the chance to develop self-discipline.

i. Homework

Homework can be a thorny issue for parents as well as children. Many parents think children in Key Stage One and Two classes are too young to have any homework, but would not challenge the school's Homework Policy, even when they have a problem persuading the children to do the work, or feel that the children need to enjoy down time after school. The ever-present fear being that the child will fall behind their peers if they do not complete additional work.

For secondary-aged children, homework can become a huge feat of organisation; getting the work done, and handing it in at the right place and right time.

Advice on homework for the older child

- ✓ Always note down homework as soon as it is given.
- ✓ Keep a separate folder for homework worksheets and assignments.
- ✓ Work regularly at a steady pace to avoid homework piling up. Working in guilty bursts is tiring and de-motivating.
- ✓ Prioritise homework each evening. This work has to be in at register, so I will do it first. I will need to get started on this tomorrow night, but I can leave that reading until the weekend.
- ✓ For extended pieces of work, record the date that work is due, then work backwards filling in other dates. Hand essay in on the 11th, proofread essay on the 9th, final write up of essay on the weekend of the 7th and so on. Organising work in reverse will avoid last minute panic.
- ✓ Keep a space free for working at home, with a collection of all the necessary equipment.
- ✓ Have friends' phone numbers to hand, in case you have a question

about the work set.

✓ Be self-disciplined. Set timed work slots for yourself, and do not use avoidance strategies.

✓ Allow yourself rewards for sustained effort. If I write out these notes for thirty minutes, I can watch 'EastEnders' and then have a bath.

✓ Use free periods at school purposefully. Work completed at school means less work to be completed at home.

j. Essay planning

For many children, beginning an essay is the most difficult aspect of the task. To help the child get started, give them a few pointers as appropriate to their age.

1. Brainstorm as many ideas that relate to the essay title as possible.

2. When you have a selection of ideas, read them through and underline the best ones.

3. Look at the question again to see exactly what it is asking you to do; then put your ideas into a skeleton of an answer.

4. You will need an introduction to explain what you are going to cover in the essay.

5. Put together a new paragraph for each point you want to make, with evidence to support that point and an explanation of why it is relevant or important.

Example. Essay title = 'Should animals live in zoos?'

1st Point. = Removing animals from their natural habitat is cruel.

<u>Evidence</u> = When in captivity, animals become lonely and exhibit anxious behaviour.

<u>Explanation</u> = Animals need company and enjoy living in extended family groups.

A new paragraph for your second point with supporting evidence and an explanation as in the example above. A new paragraph for your third point with a point, some evidence, and explanation as above.

6. It can be useful to use post-it notes for each separate point to help you to decide the order of the points.

7. You will then need to summarise your ideas and opinions in a conclusion.

k. Proofreading

Proofreading a piece of work can appear to be an irritating waste of time but is worth the effort in terms of the improvements that can be made.

Strategies to help the child to get maximum benefit from this rather tedious task:

1. To spot mistakes, it is necessary to concentrate. Switch off phones, the television, and the radio, and <u>focus.</u>

2. If work is left for a few hours before proofreading, it will be easier to spot errors. When work is re-read immediately, it is easy to read what you imagine you have written.

3. Try to focus on different purposes for proofreading. Read once to look at spelling and grammar, and then again for content and sense, checking that the correct approach, for example, the P.E.E. essay plan structure, has been followed.

4. When word processing material, use spelling and grammar checks

whilst typing to reduce the number of corrections that need to be made when the work is complete.

5. When word processing, print out a draft to proofread. It can be easier to see errors when reading from a paper copy, rather than from the screen.

6. Read the work aloud to hear mistakes or use online reading programs, such as <u>text-to-voice function</u>, to have the work read to you.

7. Check basic punctuation. Check for the correct use of commas and full stops, and consistent use of capital letters (Third reich, third Reich, third reich). When in doubt, keep sentences short.

8. If a parent or older sibling can be persuaded to read through the work, they will be in a good position to judge whether the writing makes overall sense and, if they dare, make suggestions for improvement.

9. Microsoft's <u>Spelling and Grammar tool</u>s are useful to identify more advanced spelling and grammatical errors.

10. If it is a short piece of text, scan it backwards from end to beginning to check for spelling errors. This would be too time-consuming usually, but if the text is brief and spelling accuracy is vital, reading backwards word for word will stop the brain from automatically correcting errors before they are spotted.

l. Note-taking

Some children will acquire study skills such as note-taking without any apparent effort: others will not pick up such techniques automatically.

For some children it is the need for speed when taking notes that hinders their performance. Others are thrown by the need to multi-task; they will need to listen to what the adult is saying, decide what is important, write down the main points legibly enough to read at a later date, spell unfamiliar subject vocabulary accurately, all whilst listening, sifting, and remembering further information as it is being delivered. If the child has a weak memory, they are certain to find it hard to take accurate notes.

<u>Ways to help the child:</u>

- Tell the child to be alert to important information and be ready to write when the teacher gives clues such as: 'The key issues are ...' 'In conclusion ...' 'So, for example ...' The five reasons are as follows ...'

- It might be worth telling the child to write on every other line of the page to keep their work well spaced and easy to read.

- If they use one side of the paper for their notes, they can use the opposite page for adding information later, jotting down questions they would like answered, or including examples and diagrams.

- Teach the child to use a few lines at the bottom of each page to summarise the notes on that page.

  ➢ Page 5 = Sequence of main sea battles.

  ➢ Page 10 = Summary of difficulties facing Churchill, (1942).

  ➢ Page 15 = Statistics re German army, (1939).

  Such pointers will help the child to find relevant information when flicking back through their notes. For extra clarity, the summaries could be written in a different coloured pen.

- If the child numbers the pages, it will make it easier to re-order notes if they get muddled.

- Ask a friend with neat handwriting if they would mind using carbon paper to make a copy of their notes. This will be particularly important if the child is absent. Alternatively, photocopy or take a photo of a friend's notes, or take a photo of notes from the white board to add to their file.

- Encourage the child to spell phonetically for the sake of speed, then to note down the correct spellings of any subject specific vocabulary, so they recognise the word when it is used again.

- Demonstrate the use of numbering and bullet points. Most information can be reduced to keywords and recorded in a numbered or bullet pointed list.

- Point out how to use abbreviations such as: ref, info, etc, e.g., i.e., &, + and =. The child can make up their own abbreviations for different subjects: 'Shks' for Shakespeare, 'resp' for respiration, 'eq' for earthquake and 'adj' for adjective.

m. Mind maps

A mind map is a diagram used to organise information visually. The title of the topic is written in the middle of a piece of paper and sub-topics with further details added around. All details are short, perhaps just one keyword. Boxes or circles can be drawn around important information, and images and colour added to make the information visually memorable: dates in red, battles in green, treaties in blue.

Mind maps help children to identify the main points of a topic, the essential information and show links between key ideas.

Mind maps can be used in several ways: to give an overview of a topic, to structure ideas for a creative writing task, to provide a visual image of all the information on one side of paper, or as an ongoing activity to help children to understand the relationships between the different aspects of a topic.

6. PRESENTATIONS AND PUBLIC SPEAKING

a. Giving a presentation

Many individuals find giving presentations a daunting experience. Three quarters of the UK population have a phobia of public speaking, so it would be quite normal for a child to be reluctant to deliver a talk in front of their peers. However, there are certain steps that can be taken to reduce their anxiety. The key is in the preparation.

Advice to give the child:

- Just reading from your notes will make your presentation boring. Talk the presentation through aloud as many times as possible beforehand. Practise, practise, practise, and then practise some more. The more familiar your talk is, the more confident you will feel. If you start with full notes, then every time you run through the talk, gradually reduce the notes into keyword prompts, you'll be able to recall the details from memory.

- If you practise your talk aloud, you will be able to keep speaking even if you lose your train of thought and will repeat the talk like the words of a familiar song. Run through your talk when you have a bath, in your bedroom before you go to sleep, or when you are walking home from school.

- Talking the presentation through aloud is good preparation for listening to the sound of your own voice. The talk may be perfect when you say it in your head, but when you hear your voice saying the words aloud for the first time, it will sound odd.

- When writing out notes for the talk, divide them into sections. Write down the title of each section clearly on a postcard and underline it. Against each title, note down a few keywords to act as a memory prompt for the order of points. Make these notes very clear, so you only have to glance at the card to be able to read it. Number the cards so that it is easy to keep your place.

- Time the talk. Cut out sections or add padding to ensure it is an appropriate length.

- Begin with a brief introduction to list the main areas you will cover. At the end of the talk, review the same key issues briefly by way of summary.

- Try to speak clearly and slowly. If looking at the group makes you nervous, look beyond the audience and speak to the back wall of the room.

- If you feel uncomfortable as the centre of attention, use diversionary tactics. PowerPoint presentations provide a wonderful visual distraction. The audience will be looking at the screen rather than you. Ask a friend to operate the IT, so you can feel you are working with someone else, and not performing alone.

- Pass around objects of interest that relate to the talk or encourage audience participation; perhaps by playing a game, using an audience member to demonstrate a point, or asking someone to hold up pictures. Audience participation will make your talk more interesting and divert attention away from you.

- Stick to the talk that has been planned. Do not go off at a tangent, even if things seem to be going well.

- Check your appearance before the talk. Is my nose running? Does my hair look OK? Are my flies undone? You will appear more confident if you are not fiddling with hair or clothing.

- Decide whether the audience can ask questions during or after the talk. Questions during a talk can interrupt the flow of the presentation and may be boring if the question is only of interest to one person, but input from other people can make a presentation feel like more of a discussion.

- Ask a friend to ask a few easy questions at the end of your talk; ones that you know you can answer and that will make you appear knowledgeable.

- Don't worry if you feel the presentation is going pear-shaped. Everyone will be more supportive of errors, than of a perfect, over-confident presentation. Use humour to handle any awkwardness.

b. Body Language

Speech and gesture are closely linked. It is far easier to communicate with someone using voice, facial expression, and hands, rather than just the voice. Gestures do not have to be wildly extravagant movements; even very subtle hand movements communicate meaning.

A person's body language will give away what they are thinking or feeling, even if they are actually saying something else. It is very hard to change or suppress body language, because it is so engrained in human behaviour. We will instinctively place 7% of our trust on what an individual says, 38 % on how they say it, and 55% on their body language.

Interpretations of body language that are useful for children to know:

- Lip biting = anxiety.

- Smiling = being welcoming and non-threatening.

- Eyes averted and head lowered = fear or embarrassment.

- Mirroring the body language of another person = being in agreement.

- Moving into another individual's personal space with raised voice = anger and aggression.

- Standing tall, holding head up = confidence.

- Trembling voice or holding breath = fear and anxiety.

- Foot tapping = boredom.

- Putting hands out with palms up = acceptance.

- Standing with hands on hips = expressing power and authority.

- Face touching = nervousness or hiding the truth.

Ways for children to appear confident through their body language:

- ✓ Stand or sit up straight.

- ✓ Keep their head level and relax their shoulders.

- ✓ Speak slowly and lower the pitch of their voice.

- ✓ If they are standing, stay still and keep both feet planted firmly on the floor.

- ✓ If they are sitting, rest their elbows on the arms of the chair, rather than against their sides.

- ✓ Make appropriate eye contact.

c. Body language (RBF)

It is said that communication is 7% speech, 38% tone of voice and 55% body language, therefore body language and facial expression can be considered to be essential aspects of human interaction. With regard to the above, my daughter informs me that I have a potential communication problem because of my RBF (Resting Bitch Face). She is qualified to diagnose this condition as she has the same affliction herself, often being asked by complete strangers why she is so miserable, when she is happily minding her own business and wondering what to have for lunch.

My late mother must have benefited from a similar 'don't mess with me' expression, managing to escape from a locked hospital ward (onset of dementia) without anyone daring to challenge her. She got as far as Alcatraz's car park before being picked up by security whilst hotwiring a racy little hatchback. (My mother was not some sort of badass hoodlum but had acquired a few useful life skills as a Wren driver during the Second World War.)

I'm not overly concerned about my RBF, as it serves to scare off undesirables.

Me: 'I'm sorry. What do you mean, spare change?'

Undesirable: 'Ah, forget it, lady.'

I see such talent as fair compensation for maturity, and on a par with the natural wastage that has reduced my height. I used to tower above everyone and spent my teenage years perfecting a lounge lizard slouch to avoid looking down on my latest hot date. I have now shrunk to a normal size and, since starting to teach secondary-aged boys a few years ago, have begun to feel almost cutely petite.

My weakness is probably the deafness. I've always been slightly hard of hearing but have learnt to mimic people's facial expressions when I don't quite catch what they say. Even so, my best guesses can be wildly off track. A posh independent school charity dinner springs to mind. I was seated between a Lady Some-Thing and a Major Some-Thing-Else. Lady S.T. had an incredibly upper-class accent which rendered her speech indecipherable. The pair of them were talking through me about cross-country eventing, a subject about which I know and care little, and the pros and cons of different cross-country courses. (Bit like Banger Racing, I imagine.) Then Lady S.T. suddenly let slip that she'd given up eventing herself when she'd taken up grass. I took this to mean that she was using weed, a far more interesting conversational topic than stables and stallions, and began to question her about her habit. Major Mustard registered my line of thought, and discretely corrected my mistake. Lady S.T. had not been referring to grass, as in drug, but to 'grouse', as in bird … Awkward. I put on my best RBF, sank back in the Chippendale, and downed some more Chateau Rothschild.

CHAPTER 5

EXAM SEASON

INTRODUCTION

When your children are taking public exams, parenting can be particularly challenging. You don't want to frighten them. You know that exams are not the be all and end all of life, but you also know that a good set of results will extend the range of options available to them in the future.

A fine line between carrot and stick must be tip-toed, with direction taken from the individual child. Some children may panic in exam season, and your concern will only add to their anxiety. These children will need calm reassurance. Other children may appear oblivious to the impending catastrophe, and you may need to withdraw to avoid doing GBH.

1. EXAMS AND REVISION

a. The Ultimate 20 Revision Tips for GCSE pupils.

1. Reasons to be cheerful – Part 1. You have been studying these subjects for years; even if you were not always listening, you will have been present in the classroom and are certain to have

absorbed some information.

2. Get a grip. Exams are an opportunity to demonstrate strength of character. No one would choose to revise; there are a thousand more appealing things to do, but the opportunity to exert a little self-discipline will do you no harm and is a good preparation for adult life.

3. Most secondary pupils are able to concentrate for between 30 and 40 minutes at a time. There is no point trying to revise if you have lost focus, so build regular breaks into revision sessions. When you take a break, try to do something physical: walk around the garden, run up and down the stairs, take the dog for a walk, jog round the block, or go for a bike ride. Physical exercise will increase the flow of blood to the brain and help it to work more effectively.

4. Take a little-but-often approach to revision and revisit topics occasionally during the year. The human brain is not designed to remember everything, but to forget what it assumes to be irrelevant and to retain what it feels to be useful. When information is revisited, the brain will assume that the information is of importance and memory will be activated.

5. It is worth drawing up a revision schedule to ensure that you are dividing your time between different subjects fairly, as well as pacing yourself to avoid last-minute panic. Remember that it is easy to get so involved in making a revision timetable, that it becomes an end in itself. There is no GCSE in Timetable Design. A revision timetable does not need to be a work of art, but it does need to be realistic. It would be pointless planning to revise for four hours every afternoon, if you know you are incapable of doing that amount of work in one sitting.

6. It is easier to revise when your work is in order. Sorting out your

notes is not a waste of time, but a useful revision strategy. You'll be thinking about different topics, and how they fit together. Create an index to put at the front of your files to give you the overview.

7. Work steadily. If the situation appears hopeless and you are worried that there is simply too much to do, don't think about the big picture, just plod away at small pieces. Tackle one piece of work at a time and revise it well.

8. You must <u>do something</u> with the information in order to remember it, and to avoid the 'in one ear and out the other' scenario. You will not remember facts just by reading through your files. You need to change notes into pictures, summaries, diagrams, timelines, or mind maps.

  ▪ Make up mnemonics (memory prompts) to help you to remember important facts. Mnemonics can be made from key words, for example, BIDMAS to remember the order in which to do mathematical calculations: brackets, indices, division, multiplication, addition, and subtraction.

  ▪ Run through everything you know about the characters from 'Romeo and Juliet' while you have a shower, or while you walk to school.

  ▪ Record facts on your phone, and then listen to them while walking home.

  ▪ Create summary sheets or mind maps.

  ▪ Have question and answer sessions with friends.

9. Use online revision programs and apps to add variety to your work. Although such programs tend not to be detailed, they will be interactive, likely to hold your attention, and easy to do if you are feeling tired or lethargic. The Bitesize series is a good example of a popular generic revision site. Many pupils find Quizlet useful for revising MFL vocabulary, and the CGP series of publications

for identifying the basic and essential information.

10. Word-process handwritten notes into mind maps or bullet pointed lists. Use different colours, size and style of font, and numbering. Highlight, underline, or italicise dates, characters, or specialist terms. Add images, pictures, or icons. Blu-tac these overviews to the wall next to your bed to stare at and try to memorise before going to sleep.

11. Some topics will need less revision than others. Mix sessions revising easy topics with time spent revising those topics you find more difficult. If you know that you work best in the evening, it may be a good idea to revise harder subjects at that time.

12. Make revision cards. Read the cards aloud, turn them over and rewrite them from memory to test yourself. Recite the information from memory or make new cards from the old ones. Create a list of questions from the cards and ask friends to test you on the information. See how many of the questions you can answer in two minutes. <u>Self-testing has been proved time and time again to be the most successful way to revise but remains one of the methods used least by pupils.</u>

13. It is always worth making a real effort to get to grips with understanding information. The more you understand, the less you will have to learn by rote. Take time to think about topics and how they link together, or how they are used in the real world. For example, you do not need to learn that water changes into steam when heated, because you'll already know that from boiling a kettle.

14. Explain the information to someone else, preferably someone who knows little about the topic, so that you have to be clear and concise.

15. Go back to Key Stage 3 internet revision sites or look at KS3

textbooks. Skim through these books for any pictures, diagrams, or graphs that will help your understanding. Many topics are covered in an easier format in earlier Key Stages, and re-reading books or playing KS3 inter-active internet games will remind you of the basics.

16. Look at old exam papers to see what sort of questions examiners ask. Write out bullet point answers to the questions, or practise answering them in full in the time allowed. This may seem boring but will give you a good insight into how exam questions are worded, and how long it takes to write a complete answer. There are only so many questions that can be asked about, for example, the reasons for the outbreak of World War 1. You may be lucky and practise writing an answer that comes up in the exam. Old exam papers and mark schemes are available online from all of the different exam boards.

17. Revise with others while you walk to school, go shopping, or for a bike ride. You do not have to sit alone in your room to work. Discussing the topics with friends will help you to clarify different aspects of a situation in your mind. What should be done about the Arab-Israeli conflict? What did motivate Lady Macbeth? What are the solutions to global warming? Friends may have different perspectives on issues that will add to your understanding.

18. Draw from past experience of revision. What revision techniques have worked for you in previous years and, perhaps more importantly, which techniques have not?

19. Listen to music if it helps. Some people find music helps their concentration by blocking out background noise. Music without lyrics is probably best as this will avoid the likelihood of singing along while trying to work. There is some research that indicates

pupils with a good memory can focus on revision while listening to music, while those with a poor memory are more likely to be distracted.

20. Look after yourself. Cut down on junk food. Get enough sleep and exercise. Build generous blocks of free time into your revision schedule, so you can relax without feeling guilty.

21. Steer clear of drains (anyone who saps your energy, and make you feel nervous or worried). Stick close to radiators (friends who makes you feel happy, confident, and good about yourself).

b. Exam Technique. Advice sheet.

1. Reason to be cheerful – Part 2. Fact: your paper will be marked against the other candidates' papers. A difficult exam will be difficult for everyone, but some people will be thrown and others remain calm. If the paper is hard, the pass mark will be lower, so do not allow yourself to panic.

2. RTFQ or Read The Flipping Question. Read each question slowly and carefully, highlighting any important keywords or instructions. Be alert to small words that change the meaning of a question. Check back occasionally to make sure you have not gone off-piste and started to ramble.

3. Answer a few easy questions first to get your brain into gear.

4. Spend two minutes before starting longer questions listing the points you want to make, to give yourself a framework to work around.

5. Have a go at every question. No marks will be given for blank sections.

6. Check you have answered all the questions. Check again to see if

there are questions on the back of the paper that you hadn't noticed.

7. If you are running out of time, list your final points in note form so the examiner can see where your argument was going.

8. Keep your work as neat as possible. Examiners mark hundreds of papers and having to take extra time to decipher illegible work will not bring out the best in them. If your writing is messy, write on every other line to give more white space between the words and make your answers easier to read.

9. If you are uncertain about an answer, use your common sense or make cross-subject links, for example, acid rain in Geography is the same acid rain as in Science.

10. Use all of the time available. Proofread your work, and if you feel your response isn't clear, put in a diagram to show that you have understood, but just not explained yourself very well.

11. Don't waste time worrying about the questions you can't do, rewinding to yesterday's success or disaster, berating yourself for revision you should have done. Focus on what you are doing now and do it as well as you can.

12. Once you have finished a paper, forget it and move on. Do not torment yourself over something you can do nothing about. You can do something about tomorrow's exam.

c. Exam Vocabulary

Anyone taking exams in secondary school will need to familiarise themselves with specialist exam vocabulary. This vocabulary will show the sort of response that is required to a question.

1. <u>Compare</u> = List similarities.

2. <u>Contrast</u> = List points of difference between examples.

3. <u>Compare and Contrast</u> = Identify different views on a topic, and show both similarities and differences

4. <u>Define</u> = State the precise meaning.

5. <u>Describe</u> = Give in detail the main features of the topic.

6. <u>Discuss</u> = Explain, giving different views; explore similarities and differences, draw conclusions, and give your own opinion on a topic.

7. <u>Identify</u> = Pinpoint an example or an argument.

8. <u>Illustrate</u> = Use examples, figures, or diagrams to support your argument.

9. <u>List</u> = Present concise, itemised information.

10. <u>Outline</u> = Give an overview of a subject without going into detail

11. <u>State</u> = Present in a brief, clear form without too much detail.

12. <u>Support</u> = Back up your argument with evidence and examples.

<u>d. Tests: a speed of working assessment</u>

You have exactly two minutes to complete this test, so work as quickly as you can.

1. Read all of the instructions before you start the test.

2. Write your name and age in the top left-hand corner of your paper.

3. Write your date of birth under your name.

4. Write today's date in the top right-hand corner.

5. List the exam subjects you hope to take.

6. Describe in two sentences what you want to do when you leave school.

7. Have you researched this career at all? (Yes/No answer only.)

8. Who would you go to for information about this career? For example: teacher, parents, relatives, or friends.

9. List three of your aspirations for the future.

10. Complete the first question only.

e. Extra time in exams. A time and motion study.

Following a specialist assessment, and evidence of additional support provided in school, children with individual needs may qualify for an extra time allowance in exams.

Attention Deficit Hyperactivity Disorder is one of the diagnoses that allows a child extra time in exams. Many children do not have the hyperactivity aspect of ADHD, but experience a problem maintaining concentration and focus. The general consensus is that this aspect of ADHD is more common in girls, but often goes unrecognised as the child is lost in her own little world and does not cause disruption in the classroom.

One of my daughters could be considered a prime example of the above. After leaving university, she trained as an accountant; more in the hope of a generous personal cash flow than from any deep-seated desire to join the profession. Accountancy exams proved fairly challenging because she found the subject matter tedious, and so would lose concentration. She revealed she had experienced similar problems when trying to focus during lessons she found boring at school and university. An ADHD assessment was arranged, which showed her problems with attention to be in the moderate to severe range, and more than enough to qualify for 25% extra time in her final accountancy exam.

My daughter went into this exam knowing that she would be in a separate room with other students with similar needs, away from the coughing, scribbling, and quiet sobbing of the main exam hall. It transpired that there would be only one other candidate with extra time in the room that day, a student with irritable bowel syndrome. My daughter could not have had more of a reason to be distracted. She began to create graphs recording the number of times the poor boy left the exam room, how long he was away, and whether he was going with increasing or decreasing frequency. She did manage to scrape though the exam, but the experience provided a valuable lesson in keeping one's own problems in perspective.

f. Parental Support in Exams

Exam season can be a stressful period for families, particularly if several siblings are taking exams at the same time, and their attitudes towards study are different. It will be necessary to take your lead from the child and use your knowledge of their personality to offer appropriate support.

<u>When offering help or advice, choose your moment carefully.</u>

Most teenagers find their parents irritating, so bide your time until you catch them being pleasant, then drop a pithy, but carefully worded comment into the conversation. Then retire, resisting the temptation to add more, aka, 'And another thing …'

<u>Keep your opinions to yourself.</u>

When you have tested the child for the hundredth time on coastal erosion, and you feel that with the knowledge accrued, you'd be heading for an A* / Grade 9, but the child appears to have retained big fat zippo, curb any urge to discuss this with them.

Never make comparisons.

You: 'Saskia's mother says that Saskia revises every evening.'

Child. 'Uh-huh.' (Thinks: 'Burn in hell, Saskia.')

Avoid threats.

You: 'Of course, you do realise that without qualifications, you'll end up collecting glasses at the Fox and Pheasant.'

Child. 'Uh-huh' (Thinks: 'Mmm? Hospitality work?')

Never make unconditional offers

You: 'We'll pay you £5/£10/£25 for every pass you get.'

Child. 'Uh-huh.' (Thinks: 'Will the amount hold steady, or rise in line with their sense of panic?')

It is easy for adults to make comments about things children can only learn from experience. You cannot put a wise head on young shoulders. Any adult will know the child will regret a lack of effort at a later date, but unfortunately, some knowledge only comes with experience.

There are few relationships that extend throughout life like that of parent and child. Irritation between the generations is natural, and nature's way of preparing the individual for what lies ahead.

Thirty years down the line, be certain that your children will be griping about you along with their peers:

Adult child: 'They always have their music on full blast. God only know what the neighbours think.'

Adult child: 'They are obsessed with such trivia. What they had for lunch. Who ate what and when. They have no understanding of life in the real world.'

Adult child: 'I try to have a conversation with them, but they're glued to the TV and just ignore me. Sometimes I think they don't even know I'm there.'

What goes around comes around.

2. CHILDREN BECOME THEIR PARENTS

No need for panic

On Prince Charles' seventieth birthday, his sons were asked for some personal recollections of their father. They disclosed that during family holidays in Norfolk, Prince Charles would take them out litter picking, armed with spiked poles and bin liners. William and Harry assumed this was something that all families did. However, when they started secondary school and began to pick up litter as a habit when out with friends, they soon realised that this behaviour was considered unusual, but by then the habit was ingrained.

My friend's daughter was a typical teenager and drove her mother mad with her messiness. The child's room had clothes strewn across the floor, discarded food growing mould under her bed, and windows and curtains permanently closed. After several years of nagging, my friend gave up and told her daughter she wouldn't be attempting to vacuum her room anymore because she found it so upsetting.

The daughter eventually left home to go to university. My friend entered the bedroom with a flame thrower, did the business, and then redecorated.

Time passed, the daughter finished university and moved in with an accountant called David in a bijou flat in Canary Wharf. My dutiful friend went to see the new pad, taking flowers and a bottle of wine. Her daughter asked her to remove her shoes upon entry, to put the bottle in the wine rack, and the flowers in a vase because she, and I quote, 'tried to keep her home tidy.' There was so much my friend could have said at that moment, but to her credit she resisted and murmured, 'Good for you, darling, good for you'. Uttered, I imagine, with some degree of irony, but secure in the knowledge that her domestic standards had been absorbed.

Printed in Great Britain
by Amazon

56767337R00129